PRAISE FOR *GET UP AND GET ON IT*

"My niece, Dana Frank comes from a family of entrepreneurs, whose hard work shaped a powerful destiny."

—Quincy Jones,
Music Producer

"Dana's goal in writing this unconventional business book is to amplify her voice and to help level the economic playing field."

—Daymond John,
Shark Tank

"Written in clear, engaging prose, Dana Frank weaves an inspirational tale of familial wealth generation, real estate savvy, and business advice. I couldn't put this book down."

—Dolen Perkins-Valdez,
Author of *Wench: A Novel*

"As a former chief of police, I understand the importance of empowerment and financial stability in fostering safer and more resilient communities. What sets this book, *Get Up and Get On It: A Black Entrepreneur's Lessons on Creating Legacy & Wealth* apart is its emphasis on not accumulating wealth but also on the importance of building legacy that extends beyond monetary success."

—Carmen Best, Former Seattle Police Chief
and Author of *Black in Blue: Lessons on Leadership,*
Breaking Barriers, and Racial Reconciliation

"As the founder of a foundation dedicated to empowering youth through mentoring and financial literacy, I recognize the urgency of equipping the next generation with the tools they need to succeed. Dana's book offers a roadmap for individuals from all walks of life to break free from limiting beliefs and chart a course toward prosperity. As a former NFL player, I've witnessed first-hand the financial challenges many athletes face, and Dana's book, *Get Up and Get On It*, demonstrates principles needed to change that narrative and create generational wealth."

—**K.J. Wright**, Former Professional Football Player, Founder of the Wright Way Foundation

GET UP AND GET ON IT

FOREWORD BY
DAYMOND JOHN *NEW YORK TIMES* BESTSELLING AUTHOR
AND *SHARK TANK* INVESTOR

GET UP AND GET ON IT

A BLACK ENTREPRENEUR'S LESSONS ON CREATING LEGACY & WEALTH

DANA FRANK

WILEY

Library of Congress Cataloging-in-Publication Data is Available:

ISBN 9781394198696 (Cloth)
ISBN 9781394198702 (ePub)
ISBN 9781394198719 (ePDF)

COVER ART & DESIGN: PAUL MCCARTHY

SKY10073767_042524

To my mama, Theresa Frank,

and in memory of my father, Gerald Frank

CONTENTS

FOREWORD

I had the pleasure of meeting Dana Frank, a remarkable woman, along with her son and business partner, Brett, during a privately scheduled Game Changer Meeting in the heart of New York City. Our discussion revolved around the crucial importance of using our platforms to change lives, particularly for individuals belonging to marginalized communities. Dana, with her incredible family history, shared their impressive accomplishments of a Black family building and maintaining a multi-family apartment business that began in 1950. For over seventy years, this business has supported three generations, truly showcasing their grit and resilience. Dana's ultimate goal in writing an unconventional business book was to amplify her voice and contribute to leveling the economic playing field.

It is undeniable that entrepreneurship is responsible for changing the world, as every product or service we encounter traces its origins back to someone's powerful idea. My own journey as an entrepreneur began during my childhood, growing up with a single parent who taught me the value of creativity and resourcefulness. My mother showed me the ropes of how to sew, and fashion became my passion. I started stitching and printing early logos of my brand FUBU, which stood for the acronym For Us, By Us onto various apparel items including t-shirts, hockey jerseys, and sweatshirts. What began as a small venture matured into a phenomenon as my friends and I became business partners, ultimately transforming FUBU into a six-billion-dollar company.

Before we were able to get to that point, though, we were denied bank loan after bank loan. Fortunately, my mother banked on us and took out a second mortgage on her home for $100,000. This experience taught me that passion and collaboration with family and others can empower us to achieve great things. Entrepreneurs are the driving force behind the world's progress and innovation, and I'm proud to play a part in that.

In my *New York Times* best-selling books, *The Power of Broke* and *Rise and Grind* I emphasized how entrepreneurs possess a unique perspective on the world, crafting stories of empowerment and success. Dana's account of her family's journey perfectly exemplifies this notion. Gerald and Theresa Frank, both Black individuals who grew up during the era of segregation, faced countless obstacles and discouragement due to the pre-determined narratives of defeat. However, the Frank family refused to let these perceived limitations actually hold them back. In Dana's book, she showcases the incredible resilience and determination of her parents as they followed their hearts, tapped into their creativity, and relied on their instincts to change their lives and achieve true success. Moreover, the book serves as a testament to the responsibilities and challenges of being stewards of a family legacy.

What Dana's family has achieved is not just the result of privileged trust funds. They were only able to accomplish this level of success through unwavering determination and perseverance instilled within a family working together to thrive and improve their lives and communities. This is the true essence of success, and Dana's book will provide readers with a complete and unfiltered account of how the Frank family accomplished this, along with valuable tools and insights for readers to embark on their own paths of success.

So, I ask you: How do you plan to change the world and leave a positive legacy? And more importantly, what is holding you back? What story do you listen to every day—the one that defeats you or the one that empowers you to pursue your dreams? This book aims to ignite the spark of bravery within you, enabling you to claim the abundant life you truly deserve by harnessing your strengths and talents for yourself and your family. Entrepreneurship is the key to lifelong happiness and fulfillment.

Keep grinding,

Daymond John
Founder & CEO of FUBU, "The People's Shark"
from *Shark Tank*, *New York Times* Bestselling
Author, and Investor

PREFACE

Dear Reader,

We are so glad you found this book. In it, you will uncover an extraordinary tale of resilience, determination, and the pursuit of wealth and legacy that has been the driving force behind our family for generations. We, Brett, and Taryn, are incredibly honored and humbled to introduce you to our mother, Dana Frank, and her remarkable journey chronicled in "Get Up and Get On It, A Black Entrepreneur's Lessons On Creating Legacy & Wealth."

This book unveils the inspiring story of our mother and grandmother who have been a beacon of strength and wisdom in our lives. It delves deep into the extraordinary life of our grandfather, whose vision paved the way for our family's enduring legacy. Our grandparents continually defied the odds and broke barriers, pushing the boundaries of what was thought possible for a Black family in an era plagued by racial discrimination and financial injustice.

Growing up, we witnessed firsthand the unwavering dedication and tireless work ethic of our family lineage. They taught us that wealth is not merely measured in monetary gains but in the lasting impact we have on the world around us. You will come to understand how our mother as a second-generation steward of what her parents created, instilled in us the knowledge that true equity grows through arduous work, and a deep sense of responsibility towards others.

We have been fortunate to inherit a legacy founded on resilience, and the courage to challenge the status quo. As we, too, strive to carve our paths in the world, we are guided by the wisdom passed down from generation to generation. And we shall never forget the hardship and sacrifices that this legacy took to acquire.

We encouraged our mother to share this book with the world, as it not only commemorates our family's journey but also serves as inspiration for others. To everyone reading these pages, we hope you find solace, motivation, and a renewed sense of hope in knowing that with persistence, faith, and unity, you can over-come any obstacles and build a legacy that transcends time.

With love, gratitude, and hope,
Brett and Taryn

INTRODUCTION

I am a Black woman, a wife, mother, business-owner, landlord, and property owner. The business I steward as general managing partner is already a legacy generator: I'm the second generation enjoying the fruits of the previous generation's vision and labor, and I take great pride in the fact that my lifelong work has also created a legacy for my children and future generations.

I am not beholden to anyone for anything, save the renters that rely on us to provide safe, secure, and affordable housing. I am financially independent; I make my own decisions—even if it is frustrating sometimes for my husband, who tongue-in-cheek calls me an "askhole" because I ask his opinion and then do my own thing anyway.

My business is unique: I can think of no other profession where strangers will deposit money into your bank account every month. And I'm inspired to help other Black people see the possibilities and to take the steps to invest in real estate, become housing providers, and begin to change the statistics that tell us Blacks are financially worse-off than Whites in America.

If you are not working to build a future for yourself, you are most likely supporting and building someone else's dream. You may have the desire, capability, capacity, and even means to change the narrative of your life, but something is holding you back from doing so. Are you waiting for someone else to take the wheel and fighting self-motivation? Are you too tired from your day-to-day life and find there is no time in your schedule to invest the time? Is self-doubt creeping in that you will not succeed? Are you concerned about what others might think? Or have you just bought into the tale that dictates you stay in your lane because there's less traffic?

You've been told not to color outside of the lines of life, not to draw too much attention to yourself or your ambitious dreams. Perhaps you followed your parents into their profession, or you took their solid advice and became one of the traditionally respected occupations, such as a doctor or lawyer. Even with a great degree and respected job, you still feel your paycheck is not commensurate with the hours you put in or the lifestyle you see others enjoying who seem to have a secret ingredient. Do you feel envious watching others excel as they build for themselves as you go through the drudgery of performing for someone else?

The clock is ticking. Daily, we are forced to consider the consequences of our action or inaction. Work. Rest. Work. Repeat.

Across America, only 45% of workers say they are either satisfied or extremely satisfied with their jobs (Weinstein, n.d.).

Only 20% feel very passionate about their work, while 33% believe they have reached a dead end in their career, and 21% are eager to change their careers. Older workers are the most satisfied and most engaged in their work. Younger workers are the most distressed, and they feel the least amount of loyalty to their employers. Small-firm employees feel far more engaged in their work than their corporate counterparts. Job security, healthcare coverage, and professional development are valued above additional compensation. Looking at these statistics, if only 45% are satisfied or extremely satisfied with their job, that leaves a majority who have become worker bees who live for the weekend.

It's the dread of what I call *Smonday*, when Sunday can't be enjoyed to its fullest because of preparation for Monday. The 6:00 a.m. wakeup call, followed by the routine of your morning coffee and your drive into work, which has become so robotic you don't even notice the crossing guard ushering the school children across the intersection.

We all know them. The sadness shows in their tired eyes. It is evident in their poor customer service, short temper, and lack of enthusiasm for what they are unconsciously doing. They often struggle with their weight because at the end of the day they are too exhausted to even consider physical exercise. They lack *joie de vivre* and cannot find a path out of the trenches of debt and the vicious cycle of just getting by.

We've all heard the saying that if you love what you do, you really don't work a day in your life. Take a moment and visualize what it would look like if you could create the life you desired. I'm certain for most that vision would include disposable income, more free time, less stress, and the ability to generate annuity income. Perhaps you would splurge when you travel so that when you get on an airplane, your seat would be 2A rather than the middle seat in row 28.

Doesn't the prospect of creating income that could enhance your lifestyle, even when you are not on a time clock, make you smile? How great would life be if you could make money while asleep, or better yet, at play? One of the greatest feelings is having the autonomy of being your own boss and not having your every move dictated by somebody else, the bliss of not having to worry about how you are going to pay the bills, and the security of knowing that regardless of a health emergency, family trauma, or your children's higher education. It's all covered. This feat also comes with the flexibility and freedom to take vacations when the inclement weather in your home city becomes unbearable. There would be ample time to indulge in your favorite activities: fitness, golf, tennis, wine clubs, or travel. Perhaps the dream includes a second home in a ski resort or sunny golf community. And, of course, your luxury car would take you to the finest restaurants in town. With your former paycheck, you would have settled for the least expensive item on the menu, or it would have been a matter of going into debt for special occasions. That meal you enjoyed would have long been digested, only now as you pay it off, with interest, you experience acid reflux and wonder if it was worth it.

I recognize that you may feel beaten down by a system where the odds are stacked against you, but if any part of that vision is appealing, what is holding you back?

In *Get Up and Get On It: A Black Entrepreneur's Lessons On Creating Legacy & Wealth,* I will take you behind the sometimes-messy scenes and share the successes, the grit and grind, the racism, and the hardships our family experienced and overcame in the hopes I can inspire you to ignite a flame for you and your family's future. Growing up, my father had a simple yet poignant saying: "If you don't do nothing, only one thing is for sure, ain't a damn thing gonna happen." Although my father passed away more than 25 years ago, the lessons and vision that he saw from behind his ever-present dark-tinted glasses still resonate with proven tools to create legacy. Certain lessons are timeless. Although my father's chosen vehicle was real estate, much of what I address here is universal in family businesses.

Some see investing in real estate as a gamble. To some degree, I understand; however, it's like playing table games in Vegas, and this time, the odds are in your favor. Values will rise, thus creating equity. People will always need a place to live; therefore, you are investing in a product for which there will always be demand. You will have pride of ownership when you drive by and know that you are a part of shaping a neighborhood. You will impact people's lives who live in your community. And should you decide to go into business with your family, you are creating a lifestyle and legacy that most can only envy. In what other profession can you have an investment where strangers put money in your bank account monthly? One where you can create annuity income providing one of life's necessities and be your own boss?

In these pages you'll read about the rather typical poor Black origin story of my father, Gerald Frank, and how it influenced his rather unconventional approach to building wealth. It wasn't always pretty, it wasn't always what I thought was right, but Daddy had a vision, and nothing was going to get in his way. You'll be introduced to the powerhouse that is my mother, Theresa Frank, and how together they got started in the real estate investment business—without having a down payment or a mortgage—that continues to provide for our family today.

You'll see the steps you will need to take if you take my advice and want to begin investing in real estate to become a housing provider. You'll hear me talk frankly about racism, banking while Black, being a woman in business, and the unvarnished realities of a typical day's work in the life of a housing provider. You'll get a glimpse into what's involved in the all-important process of rent collection and the complexities of tenant eviction, how the trends with rental housing laws have swung to squarely favor the tenant—even when doing so threatens to prevent landlords like me from being able to provide the very housing we so desperately need.

You'll also get to explore what it means to work with family and to create that multigenerational legacy. My family called it "passing the baton," and if you're just getting started, this book shows you how to be the first leg in the relay and pick up the baton.

You'll read about why some people are able to achieve it all, and why I know that you can too. You'll be prompted to think about giving back and paying it forward and be urged to feel the fear and do it anyway. That's what it means to be a Fire Starter.

And that's where we begin.

1

FIRE STARTERS

A Fire Starter is born with passion, drive, and vision

They don't accept the narrative at birth they were given

The life of living paycheck to paycheck and barely getting by

Waiting to collect social security when their time comes to die

Fire Starters aren't born with silver spoons or a trust fund

They refuse to be invisible and have their dreams shunned

They fight unjust systems, speak up, and protest the unfair

So the marginalized and those left out of the script will also get their share

Fire Starters' ambition is more powerful than settling for less and joining the masses

I witnessed this tenacity, grit, and grind from behind my father's glasses

My mama's DNA is a gumbo of beauty, class; she's wise, determined, and strong

My parents, my best teachers, giving lessons I was blessed to receive and now blessed to pass along

Success is earned from hard work: if you don't try, you have no one else to blame

At the end of your journey, what will be your legacy, and how big will be your flame?

—Dana Frank

My parents, Gerald and Theresa Frank, were Fire Starters. A Fire Starter is one who ignites a flame for his or her future and doesn't accept or listen to the narrative that society has given. Fire Starters change the trajectory of their own lives and hopefully that of generations to come. Fire Starters don't accept the narrative that may be based on the color of their skin, their family's economic status, where they were born or educated, or their lack of education, birth defects, lifestyle, past mishaps, poor decisions, birth order, or sex. Fire Starters create their own narratives, despite any obstacles before them, and live on their own terms.

Gerald and Theresa Frank

The most important factor is that despite all the bad cards in life being stacked against them, my parents forged ahead and lit a flame that still burns three generations later. My father, a Black child born in the Jim Crow era, came of age when laws mandated racial segregation, which invoked violence, poverty, and a melancholy existence, with a grim outlook for the future. Jim Crow was a character created by a White actor wearing black makeup meant to demean and make fun of African Americans.

My father came into the world during these turbulent and repressive times in Detroit, Michigan, on December 27, 1931. Detroit during this era was an industrial hub. The manufacturing of tanks, airplanes, weapons, and of course automobiles transported Blacks and Whites from Southern states looking for opportunity. As resentment over inequality and the economic shock just following the Great Depression rose, my teenage father witnessed the race riot of 1943. He watched his city burn as social unrest over the poor living conditions, unequal access to goods and services, and racism reached a boiling point.

My father's family maintained their home in a segregated area of town. They had a large extended community, which became like family, and they looked out for each other. There was a large contention of minorities who moved into small, subdivided apartments in an area known as Black Bottom. Violence broke out, and no White people were killed; however 17 African Americans died at the hands of police, 675 were injured, and damages amounted to $2 million (Detroit Historical Society, n.d.). The city was ravaged until 6,000 army troops arrived and the riots ceased.

Black people being beaten by the police and racially motivated killings are still part of a sad reality in our lives. We have witnessed George Floyd, Breonna Taylor, and Ahmaud Arbery—among so many others—all thriving individuals who had dreams, hopes, and aspirations, whose lives were cut short because of one thing: their skin color.

The prospect of becoming the largest Black landlord in the Central District of Seattle, owning an estate with detached guest apartments for his daughters, an in-ground swimming pool, views of Lake Washington and Mt. Rainier, driving a fleet of classic cars, raising offspring with private school educations, or traveling the world from Europe to Africa as he one day would, was as farfetched as any fairytale.

But my father never gave in to settling and accepting that where he came from was his fate.

My grandfather, Houston Frank, was a soft-spoken, kind, and gentle man who warned his ambitious son not to rock the boat. Houston suggested Gerald's other option would have been to follow the masses of his generation and look for one of the highly sought after jobs at Chrysler or Ford Motor Company. My father watched his friends go to work, exhausted, after a daily 4:00 a.m. wakeup call and a hard double shift on the assembly line, with two 15-minute cigarette breaks. At the end of 2 weeks, their paychecks were not enough to enjoy a decent meal, let alone establish savings. He watched as his grandmother saved for a year to purchase her new lemon-yellow sofa, which she covered in plastic to keep it unscathed. Each Sunday as the family would gather for one of her Southern meals, Great-grandma would yell, "The davenport is off limits!" She died having never once sat on the plastic-preserved furnishing, and it was passed along to one of her needy relatives. This was not the life Gerald Frank envisioned.

He grew increasingly sick of the disparity he was forced to live. His mother, Evelyn, was a fair-skinned beauty, with keen features and wavy auburn hair, who could pass for White. My father recalled going to a local diner with his mother and the owner berating Evelyn for bringing her chocolate-skinned child inside.

"Lady, can't you read? No Blacks allowed!" he shouted pointing at little Gerald.

On Mother's Day, when my father was 17, Evelyn, only 37 years old, died after a short illness. The loss, the plighted circumstance of his life, and limited options for better days, prompted my father to change the script and create a new narrative.

He headed to the Pacific Northwest and Seattle, nestled between the Puget Sound and Lake Washington, where he enrolled at the University of Washington. Segregation was still in effect; however, there was great promise here, the living was more tolerable than life had been in urban Detroit.

He was a budding musician, and during the early 1950s, Seattle was a boom town for the music scene. This period produced the likes of Ray Charles, and many famed musicians who performed at clubs like the Black and Tan Club and included talent like Aretha Franklin, Count Basie, Charlie Parker, and Duke Ellington, with whom my father traveled for a period. My father's first love was music, and he was an accomplished drummer and organist.

However, upon his arrival in Seattle, he found another love: real estate. My father was a quick student, and he recognized the value in owning real estate and that it would be a rapid path to earning long-term income. Music would become a side gig, and at only 18 years of age in 1950, he made an improbable decision and purchased his first investment property. My father had lied about his age and had steady work, playing drums in different nightclubs. Clubs such as Bird Land, and the Mardi Gras brought integrated crowds nightly. One night as the band took a break, my father started a conversation with a regular. The patron, a middle-aged White man, shared that he had a house for rent; however amenable he was to selling, he just hadn't found a buyer. It was a single-family home located in the Montlake area, not far from the University of Washington where my father was attending classes. My father struck a deal with the owner and acquired the property by working off the down payment. His services included maintenance work and drum lessons for the seller's son. My father was open to bartering, and he did not shy away from work. He convinced the owner to carry a contract, meaning the monthly mortgage payment of $47 was paid directly to the owner, and the owner in turn paid the bank.

My father subdivided the house, finishing the basement and creating three additional units. He rented out sections to his fellow university students to cover his expenses and pocket some income for himself.

Theresa Frank (left), Seafair Queen 1950

In 1950, my mother, Theresa Frank, who was also 18 at the time, was a stunningly beautiful young woman who had been honored by winning several pageants and crowned Seafair Queen in Seattle's most celebrated parade. The inaugural year, a queen was crowned from different nationalities. My father was playing the drums in the house band, and Mama had won Ms. Bronze in one local competition. On February 2, 1956, they married.

Mama was never one to shy away from work. As the second eldest of eight, she had always had a strong work ethic to help support her family of birth. Since she was 11 years old, she'd been holding down jobs, including being a caretaker for a wealthy family and their children. She also worked as an elevator operator, and at Providence Hospital she contemplated a career in nursing, until, while weighing diabetic foods, she was ordered to insert a man's genitals in a urinal. She decided that was not a path she wanted to pursue.

Instead, she went into her first love: the fashion industry, where she worked in Grayson's department store as a window dresser. Although she loved the work, she finally landed a better paying position at Pacific Northwest Bell. Mama's passion had always been in couture clothing, and she found lasting success as a top runway, print, and commercial model. She was always in demand to model for Nordstrom, I. Magnin, and designer boutiques, Helen's of Course, and the Mediterranean.

When she married my father, they continued to invest and utilized creative financing to acquire more property. Some tactics included leasing with an option to buy, where a portion of the monthly rent was applied to the down payment. They also crafted equity share deals, where a capital partner put up the down payment, my father was responsible for labor and improvements, and my mother handled the bookkeeping and cleaning. They would get paid for their services; thus, they created income as they continued to build. The partnership split the equity after the capital partner's down payment was returned. My parents learned early the power of networking, and they befriended entrepreneurs in the Jewish community, such as owners of the Carpet Exchange, Seattle Curtain, and Wilcoxson Hardware.

For a time, my father connected and worked for known Seattle crime boss, the late Frank Colacurcio, Sr., who was known as Seattle's longest running crime figure. Frank Colacurcio, Sr. was a Seattle strip club magnate who died at age 93 in 2010. My father connected with Colacurcio in the 1950s, and together they operated night clubs that were quite profitable. Strobe lights shone on topless dancers who lured inebriated men to give big tips. Daddy said when the city shut them down for showcasing topless women, Colacurcio reopened with bottomless acts. Obviously, that did not last long either.

Despite all their endeavors, my parents' income was meager, and my father found himself hustling. He posted a sign in the window of his truck that read: "Available to hire." Once he took it upon himself to wash windows on downtown office buildings. Upon completion of the work, he would present a bill to management. Although they hadn't requested the services, they felt obligated to pay. Once my father ordered my mother to return the peanut butter she had purchased from the grocery store because it was an unnecessary condiment that they could not afford.

By 1957, they owned a house on Helen Street, one on Thirty-second, a duplex on Temple Way, and a small six-unit complex on Washington Street. However, their promising future was brought to a halt, with my eldest sister only a few months old, when the dark narrative my father had been told during his youth in Detroit caught up with him. He was working every means he could to get ahead, and that included fast money and an alluringly fast lifestyle. Women he had met during his long weekends on the bandstand had turned against him in a furor after he married my mother, and he was busted for transporting them as prostitutes across state lines. So, he found himself sitting in jail, sentenced to 18 months at MacNeil Island Penitentiary for Violation of the Mann Act.

My mother was left to tend to her infant daughter, hold down a job at the Telephone Company, and collect rent from their rentals. When news of my father's arrest hit the front page of the *Seattle Times*, the tenants threw raw eggs at my mother when she went to collect the rent. With my father locked up, the tenants bullied my mother so they wouldn't have to pay. But Mama was steadfast and held it together as she squirreled away the mortgage notes and the $12 monthly stipend, the maximum allowance she could take my father on her monthly visit to the penitentiary.

My father's sentence of 18 months was shortened to 6 months based on good behavior. Sitting in that cell, he vowed he would change his future. My father had a choice when he reached that Y in the road. He could continue down the dead-end street of hustle or "square up," as the streets termed the act of going the straight and narrow and legitimize his path.

Upon his release, my father started living life by his mantras, "Ain't no givin' in and no givin' out" and "Get up and get on it." His stamina and work ethic were commendable. He awoke in the wee hours of the morning and felt half the day was gone for those who clocked in at nine to start their day working for someone else. He reestablished and connected with more influential business associates who became close family friends. Al Benoliel, James

Paul Jones, Richard Greene, the Capalutos, Mike Bard, Robert Wilcoxson, Woody Woodhouse, and Michael Goldfarb were some of the close-knit friends my parents engaged with as they were building their wealth. With Michael Goldfarb, who owned the Carpet Exchange, my parents partnered and purchased five apartment complexes in Capitol Hill. When the successful partnership ended, my parents bought their associates out. Michael Goldfarb was a major player and developer in the Seattle market. During the recession, he had to negotiate the restructuring of $45 million in debt. Goldfarb's assets were valued at about $113 million. My father paid attention to how his peers operated and negotiated workouts with lenders. He fought for and demanded the same opportunities allotted to them. Daddy studied every book he could get his hands on. His library shelf was stacked with titles on how to create wealth in real estate.

He taught me and my sisters the importance of continuing to educate ourselves. His constant refrain while we were growing up was, "I didn't raise no dummies. If you want to know something, open a book, and read!" He also watched the company that we kept and made sure it was with like-minded individuals. My parents practiced what they preached and partnered with some of the above-mentioned affluent friends. As their buildings appreciated, they would refinance, buy their partners out, and roll the remaining proceeds into the next building.

My father would say that when you see someone getting busy, the work ethic is contagious. One of his best friends was Benjamin F. McAdoo, the first black architect registered in the state of Washington. McAdoo was responsible for designing numerous distinctive homes in the Pacific Northwest. His mid-century modern designs inspired many of my father's renovations.

My parents started without any generational financial support, they had no formal investment training, and my father had a criminal record. But they were also equipped with a strong work ethic and drive, which has amassed a valuable portfolio beyond any of our imaginations and has supported three generations. It has supported college educations, first-class travel to exotic destinations, front-row access to experiences from the Kentucky Derby to the Super Bowl. House renovations, new cars, and designer clothes have all been made possible by investing in real estate. Real estate has been a proven vehicle time and again to create wealth. Had my father taken the job in 1950 at Ford in Detroit on the assembly line and my mother maintained her career at Pacific Northwest Bell, our lives and journeys would look markedly different.

My father and mother through all the adversity, racism, and hardship proved generational wealth was obtainable. As the steward of the company, I work to prove it is sustainable.

GET UP AND GET ON IT

- You are the only one who can change the narrative of your life and personal story.

- There should be a time limit on feeling sorry for yourself, so don't dwell on what was. Most of us—dare I say all of us—have some dysfunction from our life.

- Don't let the trauma or troubled circumstances from the past determine your future. When my father was incarcerated or my mother was assaulted trying to collect rent, they stayed the course and by doing so changed the trajectory of three generations.

- Each day, challenge yourself to be a Fire Starter. Hold yourself accountable and assess daily, weekly, and monthly what you can do to improve your circumstances.

- Work at identifying opportunities. Even if they are not actionable, get in the habit of looking for them.

- Understand in life and work, we all face obstacles. It is how you face and overcome the issues that determine both your success and the outcome.

2

GETTING INTO
REAL ESTATE

There's no place like home, Dorothy said from Oz

Warm cooked meals and family gatherings just because

Financed, finished, and furnished with style

Come on in and stay for awhile

Have some coffee; if it's late, a drink or two

The guest room is all set; yours is the room with a view

It's my most valuable asset; the equity grows everyday

And when I refinance and pull out cash, it's tax-free pay

It's the American dream where memories are created; of this, there's no debate

Tried and true, there is nothing much better than owning real estate

—Dana Frank

Real estate does not discriminate. Unlike most occupations, real estate investorship does not know your ethnicity, what college degree you hold or don't, or what pronoun you prefer to be addressed by. Once you own the property, whether it is a single-family residence, a multi-unit apartment building, or commercial space, you can manipulate your returns by renting it out, personally residing in it, sharing it with roommates, renting out all or portions of it on Airbnb for extra revenue, renovating it, refinancing and pulling out cash, selling it for a profit, or passing a valuable and appreciating asset on to your heirs.

Think about the fancy neighborhood houses of your childhood. You know, the ones you used to go to on Halloween to trick or treat, even though they weren't in your neighborhood, because they gave out the big candy bars! Peering past the entryway adorned in your sweet, silly, or scary costume, you caught a glimpse of the affluent family and their good life inside. Perhaps there was a cozy fire as the adults enjoyed hot spiked apple cider. They grinned at you knowing you weren't from their block, let alone a several-mile radius, as they tossed treats into your pillowcase or grocery bag.

If you were like me, you aspired to live that way. I wanted to know what families did to get one of those higher-end zip codes. Some were in gated communities. Some were perched on the shores of the Lake Washington waterfront with immaculate rolling lawns. Some had pools and guest houses. Missing were the broken-down vehicles parked in front. The cars with long expired license tabs, still hiked up on jacks, lining the street. Also absent were any signs of deferred maintenance or loiterers looking for narcotics or trouble. I became a student of how affluent people made their wealth, and it was apparent that real estate, a commodity we all need, was a sure and fast way to make it happen.

Our family business has primarily supported affordable housing. Affordable housing is for people who have good jobs, such as teachers, city workers, and young professionals just starting out. That is different than low-income housing. Low-income housing often involves government subsidies such as Section 8, the federal government voucher program that helps very low-income people pay for safe, private-market housing.

There will always be circumstances where renting is the right thing to do. College students, those moving to a city and wanting to learn the area before purchasing, those in transition from divorce, death in the family, or life trauma are examples of when renting may be necessary and feasible. But, when I calculate how much outflow I see from those long-term renters, paying often-escalating rent payments, there is a huge, missed opportunity for creating equity and financial growth. I once did the math, and one of our longest residing residents under lease had paid us $480,000 in rental payments over 12 years. So, even if you are forced to rent, if you see an opportunity to invest in a property, the option should be considered.

During the last 3 years of my daughter's college education, she along with four roommates rented a five-bedroom home that one of the students' parents owned. Year after year, the rent increased, and there was a line-up of students waiting to take over the lease as soon as the graduating seniors left. That was a beneficial asset for that family.

Here's just a brief list of the benefits you'll enjoy from investing in real estate and becoming a housing provider:

- Your assets will appreciate over time.
- You'll boost your monthly income.

- You'll enjoy long-term security.
- You can leverage even more investment potential.
- You'll receive tax advantages.

Perhaps you already own property, or you are just considering investing. If you already own, you're likely already enjoying the benefits of appreciation. You've heard the statistics, watched the ads for the late-night seminars, and witnessed the power of inflation at work.

Real estate will generate wealth. That home your parents purchased in 1960, when the average cost of a home was $12,000, is now on average worth $350,000. Between 1967 and 2022, housing experienced an average inflation rate of 4.23% per year. This is significant. Just ask the Federal Reserve, which strives to keep inflation at 2%. In other words, the equivalent housing that cost $100,000 in 1967 would cost $978k in 2022 (www.in2013dollars.com, n.d.).

Many parents invest in guaranteed education programs to provide a foundation for their children's future. I believe there should be programs for your children's future homeownership, a kind of guaranteed housing program, if you will. Parents with the means are increasingly helping their adult children purchase homes, whether that means cosigning a mortgage, giving money for a down payment, or buying a property outright for them. And that has a lot to do with rental prices being so high (Ballentine and Cachero, 2022).

Housing costs will continue to rise, whether you are a player and winning watching values rise, or a spectator playing more on the sidelines.

How to Start Building Your Real Estate Equity

Granted, it can be intimidating and risky to step into the world of real property ownership. However, when you consider what you are spending on leasing or renting something you don't own, those numbers are both disheartening and a strong motivator to do something differently. At least I believe they should be. Whether you're conservative or aggressive in your real estate acquisitions, real estate has proven to be a tool to provide cash flow and appreciating value over time.

Improve Your Credit Score

The first step, especially if you're just starting out, is to get your credit in shape. With poor credit, you're relegated to the sidelines of the real estate investment game. When rental applicants send over their applications for me to consider, I am often baffled at how young adults can ruin their credit in such a short time frame.

A credit report is like an x-ray full-body financial scan. A credit report lists each of your creditors and what they have reported about you. It pulls up every demerit hidden behind your poised exterior persona. That student loan that is delinquent, that cellular phone bill you forgot to pay, or the late payment to Nordstrom for the outfit you couldn't afford but had to have—all are a part of your financial DNA. The three largest credit score companies in the United States are Equifax, TransUnion, and Experian. They are required to provide one free credit report per year to consumers. You can access this free credit report on their website or by sending a request. Additionally, many banks and credit card companies now provide their customers free credit scores as part of their annual fees and maintenance.

A credit score is different than a credit report. A credit score is a three-digit number that provides potential lenders (and property owners like me) with a prediction of your credit behavior, based on your past behavior, of what the likelihood is that you'll make your payments on time. A good credit score is 670 or better. The highest score you can get is 850. Paying your bills regularly and on time and keeping your credit usage low (meaning, don't keep your credit card balance at the max of your limit and only pay minimums each month) are the things that will improve your score.

If you have a low credit score but want to invest in real estate, it's important to get a full credit report, determine which creditors are reporting negatively, and work to get those low scores removed. For example, if it's a credit card company that is reporting late payment, perhaps you can call the customer service department of the creditor and offer to pay an additional fee to remove the negative information.

The easiest type of negative scoring to repair is when you owe money to a recipient who is rightfully entitled to it. Make a payment plan, pay them on time and as promised, and ask that they remove the negative comment on your report as a condition of your repayment.

Some companies represent themselves as credit-score-repair services. I don't recommend them. They charge large fees for minimal service and often poor results.

Repairing your credit can take time, diligence, and patience. Applying for too many credit cards or other forms of credit beyond your income will lower your score. Be careful about having too many cards. And you should pay off the balance of your credit card in full every month. High-interest minimum payments will only put you further in debt and continue a cycle of poor credit.

It's also important to protect your credit as you build it. Keep an eye out for fraudulent activity by regularly checking your credit reports. If you see anything suspicious, report it to the Federal Trade Commission and your local law enforcement agency.

STOP SPENDING, START SAVING

If you have a goal of owning real estate, it means forgoing many luxuries and focusing on your goals. Consider every dollar you spend as going away and never coming back. The latte with extra cream, the vacation no matter how badly you need it, and mounting credit card charges for the new designer tennis shoes or flashy jewelry can all wait. Act your wage. I will reference many times in this book a phrase my father taught me: "Just because it's on your ass doesn't make it an asset."

If you absolutely must wear high-end clothes, buy them at thrift stores where you can get them at a fraction of the cost. You can also look at eBay, the RealReal, and First Dibs. For special occasions, you can rent that special outfit from places like Rent the Runway. There is no need to purchase a ball gown when you can rent it for a night. If you have not started saving, start today!

FINDING THE DOWN PAYMENT

Next, one of the most challenging steps is figuring out a down payment and getting prequalified for a loan. If you are gainfully employed and have been able to put away some savings, call your local loan representative or branch of any bank and find out what size of mortgage you can afford. If you already own property and it has increased in value, consider refinancing and pulling out cash for the down payment on your next investment.

But sometimes you must get creative.

Mama's signature color is white. She loves the purity of the tone on everything. Growing up, we had a white room, which Mama decorated with white fur sofas and matching bar stools. She even had a full-length skirt made from the fur that she wore at the holidays. Okay, admittedly, this sounds ridiculous, but this was the 1970s, and Mama was—and still is—a style maven. The walls of that room were painted pristine white, and the floors were carpeted in white. White, white, white. So, it was no surprise when Daddy purchased Mama a Cadillac that it was white with matching whitewall tires. Mama swore this car had an early GPS navigation system, and all she had to do was get behind the wheel, and it would take her to her destination.

My mother had fallen ill with bronchitis. After a week's worth of antibiotics, plenty of fluids, and resting in bed, Mama recovered. Now, in addition to running the business, Mama has always been the backbone of our family. Her home cooked meals, fashion sense, artistic design talents, and business acumen were sorely missed while she was sick. We had a saying in our household, "The first of the month is no time for illness," and "Got to get up and get on it." So once Mama recovered, she went outside to head to Lucky Grocery Store to replenish our food supply, only to discover her beloved white car was missing. Missing! She scanned our secluded dead-end street in a panic, seeing only our various work and utility vehicles. When she approached my father frantically screaming, he beamed, "I traded it for a view home overlooking Lake Washington. The brother thought he made a great deal, because the car could move, but the house couldn't."

My mother held a grudge until years later, when we finally sold the two-bedroom home nestled on a hill with a glorious view of Lake Washington and Mt. Rainier; we netted over $900,000. As a Fire Starter, my father understood the importance of being creative.

How can you get creative?

RENT TO OWN

If you don't have the savings for a down payment, consider a lease with option to purchase. Negotiate with the owner and increase your monthly rent, so a portion of your monthly rent goes toward the down payment. You may do a lease with option for 1 to 3 years, and at least at the end of the term you will have some capital toward the down payment.

Research programs such as Divvyhomes.com. Divvy was founded to make homeownership accessible for anyone without the privilege of generational wealth. The story of Divvy's founder, Adena, is all too familiar.

Her parents could not get approved for a traditional mortgage and only became homeowners when they were offered flexible financing by a seller. That one house provided for the family's future, paying for college education, and setting the path for their careers.

The Divvy program is a good fit if you need help with saving for a down payment, your credit score is low (Divvy requires a minimum score of 550), or you're self-employed or new on the job.

You can research other options as well:

- Home Partners of America (homepartners.com).
- Landis.com is a rent-to-own program and one of its goals is to facilitate homeownership for African Americans with low to moderate incomes.
- Dreamamerica.com. Unlike most rent-to-own firms, Dream America will consider applicants with a prior history of bankruptcy, foreclosure, and eviction, after requisite waiting periods have passed.

- Verbhouse.com. Verbhouse partners with employees of public-school systems in areas where the housing cost is out of reach relative to the income.

- Zerodown.com. ZeroDown buys a range of properties, from cabins and mobile homes to estates, and single family, townhouses, and condos.

- Orinalre.com. Original Real Estate has a unique equity enhancement program: when you make a surplus rent payment, they match 50% of that, deducting it from your home purchase price.

- Thinktrio.com. Thinktrio connects purchases with an affiliate lender who prearranges an FHA Mortgage.

These rent-to-own options are available in different states and have various approval processes (April S, n.d.).

Find a Partner

Another option is to find one or more partners. Share in the cost of the down payment and renovations, and you will find yourself making money together. Perhaps you have remodeling skills, and you have a friend who has the seed money, and you trade your labor for their capital investment. If you hold the property for a period as it appreciates, you can use the proceeds and repeat the process.

I'm not professing to follow one of those real estate hype programs that exaggerates how easy it is to go out and buy a property with zero down. I am suggesting that there are deals to be made, and you never know what someone's needs are. Spend your weekends going to open houses. Scour your neighborhoods. Talk to people, realtors, bankers, your barber, or baker. Put the word out that you are looking. Opportunity in real estate is always there. Even if you consider doing real estate investing as a side project, you will be ahead of the game.

On any employment job, your income plateau and expectation for growth are locked in. The amount of your salary, anticipated bonus, vacation time off, and sick days are set in stone. With real estate, all those variables are determined by you.

LOCATION, LOCATION, LOCATION

One must pay close attention to the economics of a city prior to investing. My father's hometown, Detroit, Michigan, was not an option for him to start his investment portfolio because it was and still is today one of the poorest cities in the United States, with a median income of $27,838. The poverty rate in Detroit is almost 38%, and the unemployment rate is close to 20%—the highest of anywhere else in the nation and more than five times higher than the national unemployment rate (worldpopultationreview.com, n.d.). Rochester, New York; Jackson, Mississippi; Syracuse, New York; Birmingham, Alabama; Springfield, Massachusetts; Newark, New Jersey, and cities in Ohio made the list with economic statistics that should make any real estate investor think twice.

Although depressed locations may have opportunities, a novice should carefully investigate and know the area prior to investing.

I have family in Detroit who did a reverse mortgage. A reverse mortgage is a financial agreement where homeowners relinquish equity in their homes in exchange for receiving regular payments, thus the mortgage rises over time as interest on the loan accrues. The area became increasingly dangerous, with break-ins and, at one point, a dead body deposited in their backyard. So, they elected to walk away from the property. The economy was so depressed that after the reverse mortgage, the home had a negative valuation.

Promises are made to restore these ravaged economies, such as Youngstown, Ohio, which was once a thriving center of steel production. On September 19, 1977, known as Black Monday, Youngstown Sheet & Tube announced massive layoffs and began shutting down. Youngstown has never recovered. Over the past decade, the city has demolished thousands of vacant homes in abandoned neighborhoods because of its decline.

Other cities hold promise for jobs and opportunities. Amazon chose Virginia over New York for its second headquarters for this reason. Virginia was rated as the top state for business in 2019, and it offered the best workforce in the nation, according to a CNBC survey, with the nation's largest concentration of science, technology, engineering, and math employees. Plus, the state ranked number one, tied with Massachusetts, for education.

According to Yahoo! money, in 2023, St. Louis, Missouri, is the top-rated city in the United States for people looking to start over. New York City is the most difficult city to move to for a fresh start. Hartford, Connecticut, has the best social scene score, while Birmingham, Alabama, has the best cost of living score compared to other cities. Pittsburgh, Pennsylvania, also ranks as one of the more affordable cities with one of the 10 lowest average rent costs for an apartment at $1,002.

Established markets already have a high cost of living and make creating wealth more challenging: cities like San Diego, California, where the average cost for a downtown apartment is $2,589 and the overall cost of living is the sixth highest across the nation—60% higher than average.

My father and mother discovered our family home late one night in December 1963. It was a small, single-family residence that sat isolated on three lots in the heart of the Central District of Seattle.

While the moon was shining over the unobstructed view of the lake, Daddy showed Mama their future home. Seattle's Chapter of CORE (Congress of Racial Equality) was fighting to integrate the segregated housing market. However, African American owners such as Myrtle DeCoulet wanted to sell and maintain Black ownership in the community. For $5,000, she was holding out for a Black purchaser, and Gerald and Theresa Frank fit that bill. Seventy-five percent of the city's nearly 30,000 Black residents lived and were confined to an area known as the Central District, and Daddy embraced the opportunity to live here. The home, with its seclusion, unobstructed lake and mountain views, permanent greenbelt, and trees, looked like heaven especially for a young man from urban Detroit. With the bonus of the proximity to downtown and equal distance from north and south Seattle, it was prime property.

For 40 years, our family assets grew, and we became the dominant Black-owned and -operated housing providers in the Central District of Seattle.

Over the years, I have invested in real estate out of my home state. I have seen the property values increase substantially where I own in Nashville and in Tempe and Tucson, Arizona, where I owned apartment buildings and our target market was college students. Without being onsite, we had to hire a property manager, which is not my preferred way to operate. We eventually sold out of our partnerships in the apartment complexes in Arizona, and I refocused on investing in properties near my home that I could drive to. My husband resides primarily in Nashville, and we are in a commuter marriage. I kept a single-family home in Scottsdale, which had been a great investment, and my family has utilized it for our personal enjoyment. During the COVID-19 pandemic, I leased the house out on Airbnb, and the nightly rate was a source of solid financial income. People were looking for safe getaway options, so investing in desirable vacation home areas with sun, golf, shopping, and activities is nearly guaranteed income. Also, finding locations that draw annual events, as in my case the Barrett Jackson auto show, which draws more than 24,000 fans annually, creates demand and high rental rates.

Airbnb was born in 2007 when two hosts welcomed three guests to their San Francisco home. It has since grown to a multi-billion-dollar company and driven wealth-generation for homeowners. If your home has a basement that you can convert to a mother-in-law unit, you may consider this a viable short-term rental for bringing in revenue.

It's a Beautiful Asset

Just because it's on your ass doesn't make it an asset. I feel the need to reemphasize my father's words here. Fancy watches, fast cars, and designer clothes will not generate long-term wealth. There will be a time to enjoy those benefits after you have invested.

Real estate is a beautiful asset, but some may need a little more work than others. Just like our offspring. But all mothers know, with their own, there is no such thing as an ugly baby. I have never encountered a property that with a little TLC (tender loving care) is unattractive. I prefer projects where I can go in and make my own improvements, creating instant equity. Some of our best and most profitable investments have been with so-called ugly properties.

Consider the fact that someone who is looking to rent a property is not making a long-term commitment. Living a year or two in an unremarkable property is acceptable with that mindset.

Time and again, the most important asset that will increase your net worth is real estate, and it always ranks in the top-performing fields of building wealth.

- **Owning your primary residence.** This kind of homeowner-ship ranks among the most common ways for people to gain a substantial increase in net worth. Instead of choosing the traditional 30-year mortgage, opt for a 15- or 20-year term so you can pay it off more quickly, which will result in significant savings on interest. If you have extra income, consider applying a greater amount to the principle.

- **The second home.** This is a savvy way to earn passive income with long-term rental agreements or via short-term rental platforms like VRBO or Airbnb. You can use the extra income to help pay off your mortgage quickly. Once the mortgage is paid off, you'll own a significant asset while still benefitting from the passive income of renting it out if you choose.

- **Rental real estate.** When you use the bank's money to acquire rental properties, you are effectively building your net worth. Once you start renting out the properties, use the income to pay off the mortgage instead of dipping into your bank account. Your properties will gain equity. Plus, their market value should increase over time. If you are not ready to acquire properties on your own, you can get a group of investors to come up with the down payment with the understanding that you'll have a percentage of ownership in the property. Once you've successfully financed the rental property, you can negotiate a fee from the investors for its management (Taylor, 2018).

My father believed in the power of reading. The books he studied were elementary enough. They told him that real estate is a sound investment. Buy low and negotiate good terms. If bank financing was not available, get the seller to provide terms with a real estate contract. In Daddy's mind, there was no such thing as an ugly building. All one had to do was minor cosmetic improvements and get an increased appraisal, then refinance and use the proceeds to roll into the next building. "Economics lessons 101," he'd say. "People are always gonna need a place to live, and I'm creating annuity income." I didn't discount my father's work ethic, and I knew he had been an excellent student. When Boeing lost contracts and signs were hung on streetlights that read, "Will the last person to leave Seattle please turn out the lights?" Lake Washington view homes were being sold for $10,000 or less. He snatched up every piece of property he could get his hands on. Our family portfolio still contains these properties seven decades later. The interiors may now have wood laminate flooring, which replaced the retro slate stone, but I still feel my father's presence when I visit inside one of our buildings.

The lesson is simple: cash erodes, and equity grows.

In addition to appreciation as the value of your property increases along with the pride of being a property owner, you will benefit from cash flow from the monthly income, reap the tax shelter benefits of deductible depreciation against your income, and you will build equity while having tenants pay down the mortgage on your asset.

However, the question looms: Do you have the grit, drive, and tenacity to take the steps and invest? Are you a risk taker? Are you ready to join the ranks of those who have the chutzpah to get up and get on it?

GET UP AND GET ON IT!

- Build and protect your credit score.

- Keep your credit score high and your debts low. Remember just because it's on your ass, doesn't make it an asset.

- Live below your means and save money for your real estate goals.

- There's no such thing as ugly real estate.

- Find creative ways to find a down payment and to get into your first property.

- Don't wait for a better market to start. History has proven that real estate goes up in value.

- Search for a deal and get creative with financing. High interest rates and a lower price on a property will result in the same effect as low rates and an escalated price, so do the math.

- Don't get stuck on turning away from a value-add property. I seek these opportunities in finding distressed properties, because handling my own renovations, I can create my own equity.

- Carefully research the economic situation in any location before you make your first real estate purchase.

3

RACISM AND RIGHTS

Once upon a time we was beaten for being black

Oh the little chil'ren they didn't talk back

They worked in the field yards every day

Picking cotton, cooking, and cleanin' and doing what the masta' say

They didn't have much joy, there was no reason to be happy

Most of 'em knew who Mama was, but where in the hell was pappy?

He was whipped and sold away without a voice

They soldiered on, they had no choice

They worked hard til theys time come to die

But the next generation suddenly asked why

They seen the white man dressing up, looking good and sharp as a tack

Tell me somebody, why am I cursed because my skin is black?

Look at all this opportunity in the so called land of the free

I want to do my thang, just let me be

Oh to wake up and see the sun risings and enjoy the fruits of this
here earth

Gonna take my inalienable rights, you know the ones given at birth

Ain't gonna be called spade, coon, or jigaboo

I'm gonna be a CEO or entrepreneur that's what I'm gonna do

Once upon a time we was beaten for being black. . .

Now we are in business, running our own and empowered to give back

—Dana Frank

The average US Black or Latino household earns half as much as a white household and has only 15% as much net worth (Aladangady and Forde, 2021).

The National Community Reinvestment Coalition released a report on appraisal bias in 2022 that showed appraisers, on average, assigned a value that was $7,000 higher to the same home when a white homeowner opened the door rather than a Black homeowner (Lilien, 2022).

Homes in Black neighborhoods are valued up to 23% lower than what their valuation would be in non-Black neighborhoods (Rothwell and Perry, 2022).

The homeownership gap is widening, and Black homeownership is dropping. In 2022, 74% of whites owned homes compared with 45% of Blacks (Henderson, 2022).

Like me, you have probably witnessed or experienced these demographic inequities. My husband, although he was born on the East Coast, now lives in Nashville, Tennessee, where I live part time. I have also spent time working in Newark, New Jersey, and I have traveled to nearly every state, from Illinois to California, Texas to Florida, from west coast to east coast. Especially in the South, the disparity between Black and White neighborhoods and property values is evident.

Dealing with and facing discrimination is something Black people in America have been dealing with since there were Black people in America. Yes, some things have changed, and some things are better than they were. But in 2019, I was reminded just how pervasive the issues around racism still are.

I was at a friend's December holiday party when a well-known White person arrived in blackface makeup with a curly wig. Being one of the few minorities at the gathering, I made my way up to this individual, wondering if maybe he might be suffering from a skin disorder. When I discovered it was clearly dark makeup smudged over his pale skin, I was taken aback.

"Why are you dressed in blackface?" I asked. "It's not Halloween, and even if it was, this is totally unacceptable."

The drunken party guest tried to defend his position, saying that the night of the gathering, December 8, was Sammy Davis, Jr.'s birthday and in honor of that he was dressing up as one of the Rat Pack. The rage boiled in me as I tried to educate this privileged, successful White man on the ignorance of what he was doing. Our hosts were mortified. They asked this insensitive and irresponsible guest to leave, and to my knowledge, they have not invited him back.

BOTH SIDES OF THE EQUATION

My modern-day experience helped me better understand what life was like for my parents, who were Black and broke—but not broken. Had my father accepted the discriminatory bias and the script that the times designed for him and stayed in the confines of the system, he most likely would have wound up working at Detroit Edison like his father.

My entire life, I have been privy to both sides of the equation, meaning the haves and have nots. I'm a Black woman raised in the Central District of Seattle. You know what they say: you are in the 'hood if you live near a street named Rosa Parks Ave. or Martin Luther King Blvd. I was raised within walking distance to MLK Way.

I'm a proud product of my roots and believe I benefited from *not* having been sheltered from life. As I walk by a downtown corner, headed to the home of a local billionaire for dinner, my name may be called out by a crack addict who used to work for my family asking for a handout. In Seattle, gentrification is real, and there is no defining dividing line between opulent neighborhoods and homelessness. Downtown Seattle's demographics have changed dramatically with increased drug consumption activity, and it is not uncommon to see the homeless seeking shelter, even in the passageway of multi-million-dollar condominiums or near five-star hotels such as the Fairmont or Four Seasons. I have spent nights going on search-and-rescue missions with our Union Gospel Mission agency seeking these lost souls and providing food, water, and staples. I have witnessed that Blacks are overrepresented in Seattle's marginalized groups.

When visitors come to Seattle, they often ask, "Where are the Black folks?" Seattle in the 1960s had one Black person for every 20 residents. Compared to other US cities, our Emerald City, Seattle, still has a low Black population: less than 7% (Balk, 2020). In our gentrified Central District, housing values have escalated, and many Black families have sold their homes and moved further south in the region.

While growing up, I did not go to the same local public schools most of my neighborhood peers attended that had a higher diverse population. Instead, it took 45 minutes on two busses—number 27 and then a transfer to number 48—to get to my private Catholic high school. The high school was all White, except for five other minorities. This was during the 1980s when disco was said to suck and the powerful TV miniseries, *Roots,* where Alex Haley's family history was followed from West Africa through slavery, prompted some hot and heavy discussions. It was the first time that the hideous visual story of the deep pain, torture, and hardship that any Black person felt embedded in their own family roots came to life.

It was unsettling, infuriating, and humiliating being the only Black student sitting in my second-period history class as we reviewed the poignant television series. Some of my White classmates joked and called each other Kunta Kinte, Kizzy, or Chicken George, all names of the enslaved ancestors of Alex Haley.

Once, a group of my classmates running to a friend's car after school shouted, "I'm not riding nigger," which meant they would not ride in the backseat. There were always apologies, after my forgotten presence was acknowledged. However, the racism was deep and inbred. The fear and loathing of the Black community was even more evident when our sports team played against schools such as Garfield, Franklin, or Cleveland, which had the highest Black student bodies. I was a cheerleader, and our squad was often cheering to empty bleachers, as our classmates were too afraid to venture into the 'hood.

My father wouldn't allow us to be silenced by White ignorance. Like the time my sister's locker had a sign posted on it that said, "Only niggers sell chocolate" during our annual candy sale fundraiser. Daddy insisted that an assembly be held in our school auditorium to honor Dr. Martin Luther King Jr. Day, which was not a school holiday back then. Even though the school had not acknowledged the holiday, our mother would insist we take the day off, and then she would write an absence note saying that we stayed home out of respect for Dr. Martin Luther King, Jr.

One night in early December, I was 16 and had just started driving. I arrived home to find my mother and our extended family gathered in our family dining room. Men in blue greeted me as a dozen police officers raided our home. In my father's absence, our home had been dismantled with every drawer emptied on the floor, plants dug up, and the entire house in complete disarray.

The search warrant said they were looking for drugs. Although none were found, they left with my mother's jewelry, which had been locked in a safe. They had demanded the code to the safe during their search and refused to allow my mother to be present while they absconded with her items. The next day after the damage was done, a call came from the police chief that they had raided the wrong house.

In the early 1980s we didn't have the Black role models that we have today. There was no Oprah, Michelle Obama, or Stacy Abrams who were living examples of Black excellence to refute the preconceived notions that as Black people, we were somehow less than. Our Black community needed representation, and we had emerging stars, but mostly in the pop art, music, and sports genres. A Google search of famous Black people of the era will produce Mr. T, Gary Coleman, Eddie Murphy, Prince, Ice T, and Bill Cosby. We had not yet had a Black president in Barack Obama nor a Black vice president in Kamala Harris. We had Michael Jackson, one of the most talented artists of our era, who no longer resembled the little Black boy from Gary, Indiana. We had Whitney Houston, in my opinion the most powerful voice of my generation, who was accused of trying to appeal to White America. Years later, when Whitney married Bobby Brown and succumbed to the shameful downfall of drugs, alcohol, and financial ruin, the tabloids and press had a field day, engaging in schadenfreude, a German word meaning to take pleasure in another's misery. Schadenfreude was also evident when the first Black Miss. America, Vanessa Williams, was forced to resign after photographs of her were published in *Penthouse* magazine.

My neighborhood, in stark contrast to my school, was a multicultural gumbo. On our dead-end street, my Black family by any standard would be considered affluent, but it was a hard-fought measure to gain our wealth. We never felt the need or desire for so-called White flight, the process of establishing wealth and making a move to suburbia. This is often the case with professional Black athletes: when they sign their juicy contracts, they move as far away as possible from streets named MLK.

I often hear people say, "We didn't know we were poor growing up." By the same token, I never knew we had means. Perhaps it is because our parents instilled a work ethic, and we never felt a sense of entitlement that sometimes comes with a birthright. We were not an upper-class African American family who joined elite Black organizations such as the Links or Jack and Jill, and we didn't attend debutante balls. Our home was an open house to the last, the least, and the lost from all walks of life, particularly those seeking my father's knowledge.

I was also nurtured by three White families who taught me White culture and from them I learned to ski, swim, camp, drink TAB, and to love graham crackers. Unlike many of the White families I met in high school, my White neighbors were civil rights activists, philanthropists, diversity, equity, and inclusion champions, even before DEI (diversity, equity, and inclusion) was a household acronym.

I loved to visit a lady named Anne Gerber. The Fair Housing Listing Service, which worked on the issue of minority housing, was founded by her husband, Sid Gerber, a Jewish man who died in a plane crash. Annie, as I fondly called her, exposed me to the arts and took me to Bumbershoot, Seattle's annual arts festival. She opened her house daily for me to wander among her sculptures and paintings and I learned to swim in her indoor pool. That early exposure instilled my love of art.

Another key figure in my upbringing was Mrs. Winsberg, a German lady who hosted a weekly story hour. We read books previously unknown to me or my family, like *Moby Dick* and *Pippy Longstocking*. I was fond of *Island of the Blue Dolphins*, perhaps because the character was an American Indian woman and there weren't many books in the era with brown girls like me.

Aside from my parents, the most impactful people in my upbringing were my surrogate mom and dad and best friends' parents, Ed and Joan Singler. Joan, a White civil rights activist from Detroit, was one of the authors of *Seattle in Black and White*. She and Ed were also founding members of Seattle CORE (Congress of Racial Equality). By the 1960s, our Central District had morphed into the heart of the civil rights movement in Seattle. Their campaigns fought employment and police discrimination, school segregation, and unequal housing opportunities. When I think of the Singlers, who at the time of this writing are well into their 90s, I credit them with teaching me that we all must be a part of changing the narrative for those left out of the script.

In addition to their civil rights activism, Joan and Ed exposed me to compassion, adventure, and concern for our environment. They took me camping, skiing, and on weekends, Joan would have all the kids grab a garbage bag and do a neighborhood trash pickup in exchange for a Popsicle. I owe a huge debt of gratitude to these families for their insights into racial inequality and the fact that it is not just a Black person's fight. Joan and Ed would champion grocery store strikes when they wouldn't employ Black people. They held picket signs and fought systems that were unjust and unfair.

When I was a child, money was never a factor in our neighborhood. We were fearless, roaring down Yesler Street on the go-carts my father's maintenance men constructed for us with wheels off local grocery store carts. We rode bikes, roller skated, and entertained ourselves until dinner time when our mothers would yell from the front porch that it was time to come in for dinner. We didn't have cell phones, computers, Xboxes, game boys, or social media to entertain us. If trouble found us, any neighborhood parent had the authority to reprimand us. The punishment could be a whipping with a branch from the nearest tree, neighborhood garbage cleanup, or a timeout, depending on which parent caught you in the act. We all survived and graduated high school and went our separate ways.

BLACK AND BROKE IN AMERICA

Fast forward more than four decades later, and when I compare the disparity of wealth between most of my Black and White friends, the inequities are evident. Many of my Black friends have died from drugs, AIDS, suicide, alcoholism, or gun violence. Some have turned to the street life and spent years in prison for crimes from auto theft to pimping. And sadly, this cycle of life continues for many of their offspring. By contrast, most of my White friends have attended prestigious schools, own luxury homes, and are members of elite clubs and organizations.

What was the defining Y in our roads that made our destinations and experiences in life so different? I respect that for many their lives are content; however, I'm addressing a national picture for those who feel they cannot break the poverty cycle and lay a foundation for their offspring.

The statistics I started this chapter with are even more dismal when we see that 64% of Black households are fatherless and the disproportionate amount of African American men who are incarcerated.

We must change the narrative. Period. As I shared earlier, my father did not allow his imprisonment to stop him from pivoting.

Let's face it, it is tough to be Black and broke in America. I am a Black mother, and I am horrified by the countless deaths of our Black youth at the hands of police. The disproportionate number of incarcerated African Americans as of 2022 is nearly 40%, although we are only 13% of the population (Wessler, 2022), and an estimated 64% of Black households are fatherless (Annie E. Casey Foundation, 2022), which attests to the fact that it does take a village to raise a child.

While we work on reform, I am advocating education as well as creating more opportunities for marginalized communities. If poverty is a disease, how do we cure it? Let's get a prescription started and stop the cycle of generational poverty and create opportunities.

Racial inequity, gender bias, profiling on mental health, harassment, and systemic discrimination must cease to exist if we are ever going to level the economic and social playing field.

In our rental business, the face of our typical applicant has changed. As gentrification has taken place, properties that my parents purchased and were once in historically all-Black neighborhoods are now a multicultural melting pot. We have a large demographic of transgender and nonbinary residents. This is the world that I want to live in and that is one where everyone is accepted and allowed to be themselves. We have zero tolerance for hate crimes and residents who do not respect those who reside in their community. Perhaps it was my upbringing being the minority in an all-White school and knowing what it feels like to be an outsider which makes me hypersensitive to this issue. We should embrace each other's differences. Why hate on something someone cannot change?

GET UP AND GET ON IT!

- Diversity, equity, and inclusion is a practice we should all live by. Embrace, respect, and appreciate that everyone has a right for fair treatment. Equality should be taught early, and exposure is key.

- Racism is learned early. Children live what they learn, so be cautious of allowing them to inherit your inherent prejudice—and if you're Black, this includes being aware that you may well have a bias about White people. Do you want them to pick that up?

- Understand that disagreements over religion, politics, race, skin color, and preconceived prejudice are rooted in ignorance. Think back to your first encounter where you witnessed someone being discriminated against something they cannot change. I once had a Black, male, gay, adopted young man say to me, "Do you think I would choose these titles? It's who I am." We need to all understand and embrace diversity, equity, and inclusion if we are ever going to level the economic playing field and create a world based on skill set and not bigotry.

- Know your rights. If you feel you are unjustly discriminated against, speak up to the authorities and file a complaint.

- Words matter, so use them cautiously. The words *encourage* and *discourage* both end the same way but have a drastically different outcome. Let's always encourage each other.

4

BANKING WHILE BLACK

Dear Banker

You are like the Grinch who stole Christmas every year

Without access to lending how are we to persevere?

The racial borrowing inequities are clear before our eyes

Denied at twice the rate of white applicants, we will not tolerate any more lies

Buy real estate, work for equity, to prosper, it's a must

But whose name is on the Deed of Trust?

Banker, we need a partner to create long-term wealth

As hard as I try, I can't do it by myself. . .

—Dana Frank

Theresa Frank circa 1965 headed to the bank

It's no secret that it is more difficult for Blacks to secure financing in America. Historically, banks have been cited for discriminatory practices, including not granting loans in certain neighborhoods based on racial demographics. Blacks are several times more likely to be unbanked, without a primary checking account, and they are more likely to rely on high-cost financial services like payday loans and pawn shops (Broady, McComas, and Ouazad, 2021).

REDLINING

My father, along with friends like Benjamin F. McAdoo, opened doors especially where housing was concerned. He participated in a project called Operation Window Shop. It was a day set aside for Black buyers to look outside of the Central District for housing. When real estate agents found out Blacks were touring, they closed all the open houses. Mortgage companies and banks denied property financing applications from them and realtors wouldn't show properties for sale or rent to people of color in specific neighborhoods, which promoted housing segregation.

It was a discriminatory practice that became known as "redlining." In the 1970s, civil rights advocates painted a red line along 14th Avenue between Yesler Way and Union in Seattle's Central District to protest the restrictions on where people could buy, rent, or get bank financing based on race and ethnicity (Honig, 2021). It helped to expose the region's race wars and encouraged some White owners to sell to Black buyers.

The properties my parents acquired were located directly in the redline zone. Banks wouldn't lend them money, so my father had to get creative, be it zero down, partnering with a White bankable person, working off the down payment, or having the owner carry the financing. By 1969, my parents owned a multi-family property on virtually every block in the Central District, from Thirty-third Avenue to Tenth Avenue, without ever having received financial assistance. A monumental success. Their first loan, secured through Black-owned Liberty Bank, didn't come in until 1969—a full 19 years after my father's first property purchase through a creative financing arrangement. My father remodeled these properties, as he said, so Black people could live with dignity. He also did so to create wealth for himself and our family.

PROPERTY OWNERSHIP BY BLACK FAMILIES

And while some things have improved, Black families continue to fall further behind in property ownership. I see this in the population I serve in the rental community.

- Black applicants seeking loans are charged higher interest rates than Whites and have a greater percentage of mortgage denial (Choi and Mattingly, 2022).

- In 2022, homeownership was 74.6% for White households compared with 45.3% for Black households, a gap of more than 29 points.

- In 1960, the White homeownership rate was 65%, and the Black rate was 38%, a 27-point gap.

- In 2019, Black homeownership fell to 40.6%, down from the 2004 peak of 49.7% and advocates remain dismayed at how decades after the 1968 Fair Housing Act that Black families still struggle to become homeowners at the same rate as their White peers.

- The persistence of redlining, the Great Recession, gentrification, and the increasing number of homes being scooped up by investors all have contributed to the growing homeownership disparity between Black and White, which is larger now than it was in the early 1960s (Henderson, 2022).

- Even among millennials, the homeownership rate, at 60%, lags behind older generations at the same age. Apartment list reports that 65% of Gen X (anyone born between 1965 and 1980), 80% percent of baby boomers (born between 1946 and 1964) own, and 73% of the silent generation (born between 1928 and 1945) owned homes at age 40 (Leidy, 2023).

CLOSING THE GAP

Washington, D.C., Mayor Muriel Bowser has unveiled a plan that aims to add 20,000 Black households to the ranks of that city's homeowners by 2030. "We know if we can close that gap, we can increase Black wealth in our city, and we know that is the way to pass down generational wealth," she said. I could not agree more with the mayor's statement. These wealth gaps persist across generations because minority households are less likely to receive intergenerational transfers from their parents (Bowser, 2022).

If banking institutions fulfill their commitments to broaden the financial gap, the future will look markedly different for all. If my father had not made the improbable decision as an 18-year-old Black man and purchased his first investment property in 1950, I would not be a witness to or a beneficiary of the power of real estate.

THE SEARCH FOR FAVORABLE TERMS

"If I'm drowning and you can't swim, leave me the fuck alone, and get me to the president of your branch," my father had said in 1984 during one of his heated phone call negotiations with bankers.

Our family business was financially near ruin. My father had been using rental income to renovate units, which should have been for paying the mortgage and recurring monthly bills. This was prior to gentrification of the Central District, and he was over-improving units where the neighborhoods could not justify the rent. He believed that his fellow Black residents deserved quality housing, and he reasoned if he fixed the property up and increased the value, he would be able to recoup the investment. Murphy beds would emerge from hiding in the walls of studio apartments. Stone or slate floors would be installed rather than inexpensive hardware linoleum, which stained or ripped too easily. He had the exterior of the buildings painted in bold tones, modeled after town homes he'd seen on a trip to San Francisco's Embarcadero District.

My father also began customizing automobiles for resale. He'd scan the classified section of newspapers looking for Seville Cadillacs, then buy and customize them to add a convertible top or a rumble seat to the rear.

The real estate renovations and automobile expenditures were putting the family business in arrears. Payments to Seafirst Bank, which carried mortgages on several notes, were past due. Frank Enterprises was going to have to double up payments to Seafirst and that would leave the other properties as well as utilities and taxes in default. Our family business was in dire need of a cash-out refinance. A refinance, or refi, is a process of revising the terms of an existing mortgage or loan, which can include favorable interest rate reductions, payment schedules, or pulling out cash based on equity in your property.

Daddy put on his chocolate-brown double-breasted suit the morning of his scheduled meeting. He adjusted his tie in the mirror and gritted his pearly whites.

Mama rushed up the stairs in her white gabardine suit with navy trim. "So, Gerald, how are you going to handle this meeting today? I don't think attacking them is the solution," she said.

"Don't tell me how to handle my business. Until you can come up with a reasonable solution that will work, instead of criticizing my plan, I will take care of it."

"Don't insult me. This is not just your business. I've invested nearly 30 years helping you build it, and I'll be damned if I'm going to sit back and watch it disappear."

The doorbell signaled the arrival of the bankers, and my mother went downstairs to let them in. Mr. Walker, our housekeeper, seated them in the dining room and offered coffee service. My father kept them waiting.

After 20 minutes, Daddy whistled down the stairs and joined the group at the dining table. "Now, the reason I have called this meeting is to inform you that I want to be treated like all the White millionaires. I can't imagine Donald Trump being treated the way I am. My business is continuously operating in a deficit because your lending practices still redline and won't allow me to bring money into this community."

The president, whom my father had insisted attend this meeting, sent two bankers in his place instead, one White and the other an obligatory minority, an Asian, who lived in Lynnwood, a White suburb of Seattle. The bankers argued that although we had ample equity, our financials showed losses because we reinvested our profits into improvements. It was the same familiar rejection and excuse.

My father asked the Asian banker how many Blacks or Asians or people of color lived on his block. When the banker responded, stunned, that he didn't see the relevance, my father said, "My point exactly. You feel it is okay to move to some lily-white neighborhood and forget your ethnic responsibilities. I was born Black, raised Black, gonna die Black, and if there's reincarnation, I'm gonna come back Black. Therefore, it is my responsibility to house Black people! I just can't run and hide in Lynnwood, a White man's suburb!"

I joined my father, and we escorted the bankers on a tour of our properties to show them the improvements underway. I used my master key to open the security door, and we walked the two bankers through the long cold corridors with heavy knockdown wall texture, chipped popcorn ceilings, and dull fluorescent lighting. Our footsteps echoed on the gray cement flooring. As we passed each unit's door, the sounds of the Section 8 subsidized and welfare babies bellowing competed with blaring television sets. Daddy looked at the bankers, shrugged his shoulders, and said, "If I don't house these people, who will?"

The strong aroma of Southern cooking permeated the poorly ventilated hallways. Daddy knocked at unit 202, a recently remodeled apartment he had painted in a yellow and black theme. Velma, with her three babies all under the age of five, came peeping around the corner when the door opened.

"Good morning, dear," Daddy said in his most charming voice. Velma looked startled to see her new landlord. The scarf tied around her head did not hold in all her hair rollers, and she pulled one of the detached pink Styrofoam pieces out. "These uh, bankers here want to talk to you about relocatin' to Lynnwood. You see, they cut off my funding, and I can't afford to keep goin'."

Tour over and the bankers seeming unimpressed, my father reverted to his old, unconventional methods of exposing the injustice. He put pickets on the bank branches and the bankers' private residences. He shared his complaint in the press and continued to amplify his discontent. By the fall, Seafirst Bank had negotiated a less than desirable compromise.

My father's pleas for an approved refinance loan with cash back fell on deaf ears. When the bankers' decision came, my father called a family meeting sharing that he was not the least bit satisfied with the outcome of negotiations with the bank; however, his hands were tied, and there was nothing that he could do. The terms of the loan agreement stated that Frank Enterprises would set up a semi-receivership where tenants paid all their rent directly to the bank. The mortgages would be withdrawn on a preauthorized transfer, allowing the delinquent payments to be tacked on to the end of the loan. The cash-back element wasn't enough to continue the progressive renovations, but it did stave off foreclosure.

I had long heard stories of and experienced racial bias in lending. Thirty years later, I too was given a loan with disbursement restrictions. The proceeds of my loan had to be held in the bank account and released as the banker saw fit to give me draws after he inspected our renovations. I, like my father, felt like I was being controlled and not trusted to govern my own finances. The irony for me was that the building showed enough equity to pull out the capital, and it was a loan of less than 50% loan-to-value (LTV). LTV is an often-used ratio in mortgage lending that determines the amount that can be financed. For example, a property valued at $100,000 with a $70,000 loan has a 70% LTV. Generally, an 80% LTV ratio is good. However, my money was held under bank control while I was still required to pay the monthly interest and payment down. Essentially, I was granted a loan that I did not have ready access to until a bank representative inspected my draw request. It was both infuriating and humiliating.

Another time, I was seeking to refinance a triplex with JPMorgan Chase. The existing financing had an undesirable interest rate, payments that I was looking to lower, and I wanted to replenish some of the cash I'd just spent renovating the complex. I had invested substantial capital in improvements: a new roof, deck, exterior paint, and interior unit upgrades. I had the appraisal completed, the property had positive cash flow, and it was in a trendy neighborhood with a low vacancy factor. The tree-lined streets were filled with new construction, and million-dollar-plus properties were being occupied by the ever-changing gentrification in the area. My parents had purchased the property in 1969, and I watched as the neighborhood morphed over the years into one of the most sought-after locations in which to live.

The loan was low risk for any bank. There was ample equity: the property was financed at only 30% LTV. In addition to the low LTV, the upgrades, the cash flow, and my quality credit score, I had north of seven figures on deposit in their branch. However, my refinance request to lower my payments with a preferred interest rate was turned down.

How was I to grow my business without my bank in my corner? I see this time and again with many minorities seeking funding. Therefore, the question begs, how do we bridge this financial gap and educate our youth, particularly those of color, on creating generational wealth and making it accessible, when this institutional bias against Blacks and other minorities persists?

CHANGE IN THE AIR

On October 9, 2020, my son had shared an article with me written by Ken Sweet and Alexandra Olson of the Associated Press, titled, "JP Morgan Pledges $30B Investment to End Banking's 'Systemic Racism.'"

The article confirmed what I had long experienced and known: banking while Black is a struggle. The bank was admitting to its long-held partiality with a commitment of $30 billion over the next 5 years toward programs that include earmarking more money for getting Black and Latino families into homeownership and providing additional financing to build affordable rental housing units.

The Biden administration has set up a task force to combat redlining and more and more cases involving alleged discrimination by financial industry players are finding their way into the courts.

In one of the largest redlining settlements, City National Bank—just one of the latest banks to be found systematically refusing to lend to racial and ethnic minorities—was required to pay more than $31 million. The Justice Department says that between 2017 and 2020, City National avoided marketing and underwriting mortgages in majority minority communities in Los Angeles County (Associated Press, 2023).

The good news is that with the lawsuits and exposure of banks denying loans to minorities, more programs are now available to help Blacks and other minorities secure financing.

Bank of America launched the Community Affordable Loan Solution, a new zero down payment and zero closing cost to help predominantly minority communities buy their first homes. Eligibility is based on income and home location, and the bonus is that there is no minimum credit score or private mortgage insurance, which is coverage for the lender against loss in case of default by the borrower.

U.S. Bank launched U.S. Bank Access Commitment, a long-term approach to help build wealth while redefining how to serve racially diverse communities and provide more opportunities for racially diverse employees. U.S. Bank started with the Black community because that is where the persistent racial wealth gap in the United States is the largest (U.S. Bank, 2023).

In the aftermath of the police killing of George Floyd, JP Morgan Chase announced a commitment of $1.75 billion to help address racial inequalities. Citibank announced it was committing $1 billion toward closing the gap in the United States, including $550 million toward homeownership programs for racial minorities. J.P. Morgan has $3.2 trillion in assets and said it expects the $30 billion commitment to help finance 40,000 additional mortgages for Black and Latino households and an additional 20,000 loans that will refinance and help construct 100,000 affordable rental units. Additionally, funds will go to finance 15,000 small business loans to Black- and Latino-owned businesses.

Twenty-seven major New York–based financial companies like J.P. Morgan joined together in a program to recruit 100,000 workers from the city's low-income, predominantly Black and Latino communities over the next 10 years. MasterCard announced a $500 million investment in Black communities, and IBM is investing $100 million in technology education at historically Black universities.

These measures should not be in the news only in the face of tragedy, however, but every day until the racial inequity is leveled. As these and other opportunities avail, community members must aggressively apply. Advocates must understand and vocalize the need for these programs. We need more education, DEI training and enforcement, and we need to hold banking and systems accountable. And Black businesses must demand a level playing field and a seat at the table.

WHERE ARE THE MINORITIES?

My opportunity for a seat at the table, ironically, landed me at a luxurious CEO forum in January 2023 in Park City, Utah, shortly after JPMorgan Chase, the event sponsor, had committed $350 million to grow Black-, Latino-, and women-owned small businesses. This was the same bank that had refused my request for a refinance of an existing Chase loan.

But as I sat in the opulence of this event and looked around the room, I had one question: Where were the minorities JPMorgan Chase had committed to help? I am accustomed to being the only Black woman in rooms like these, but it was incongruous. The global co-head of mergers and acquisitions is Asian. Her biography is impressive, with domestic and international clients on close to $1 trillion worth of transactions. Her biography shares that she is involved with several initiatives across J.P. Morgan and Wall Street to recruit, mentor, and develop women. Aside from her, I am one of only a handful of people of color in attendance. Although she was not affiliated with the department where I needed assistance, I wish I had known how to reach her when my Chase loan had been denied. Perhaps she could have directed me to some of the programs previously listed. I was certain no matter how challenging the road to building wealth was for the CEO attendees at the Park City Chase Bank conference may have been, the struggles did not compare to financing while being Black. "White Americans hold, on average, almost $1 million in family wealth compared with an average of just $143,000 for Black Americans" (McIntosh, Moss, Nunn, and Shambaugh, 2020). This figure equates to less than 15% of White families' totals.

While in Park City, I sat by the cozy Stein Eriksen lodge fireplace and read New York Times writer Emily Flitter's book, *The White Wall: How Big Finance Bankrupts Black America*. The book cover was enough to cause discomfort among the conference attendees. In the book, Emily exposes discrimination against BIPOC in bank financing. She digs into the deep-rooted racism in the banking industry. The book details how bank practices have kept the racial wealth gap in effect and proves that what my parents had fought for was indeed worth the battle. The author writes about how Black former NFL player, Jimmy Kennedy, who earned $13 million during his 9 years in the league, was denied private client status normally offered to clients earning $250,000 essentially because he was Black.

I have countless White friends who have significantly less net worth than Jimmy Kennedy, and this status has been extended to them.

Kennedy's story struck a nerve for me. As I reflect on the Black professional athletes I have personally known and the masses that I have read about who had an opportunity to leverage their large, albeit short-lived salaries and have lost it, it is tragic. These young, gifted sports stars have spent their lives training their bodies, when it should also be a requirement to educate their minds on investing. Unfortunately, far too few ever trust a third-party professional with their finances. Due to poor investment management, some of these former athletes have lost their fortunes, family security, and sadly their future legacy. On average, 3 years after their professional athletic life is over, they are broke. Mike Tyson racked up $23 million in debt, including $13.4 million to the IRS (TSL Contributor, 2022). Floyd Mayweather at one point owed the IRS $22.2 million. These are examples of Black athletes who did not have the knowledge or guidance to capitalize on a tremendous financial opportunity.

In the 1980s, as a young real estate agent, I tried to broker the sale of a 16-unit apartment complex to a celebrated NFL star. At the time, his salary was more than $1 million a year, and financing would not have been an issue. The asking price for the 16-unit complex was $750,000. His agent rejected the proposed purchase. Today that same building is worth more than $9 million and the former ball player is destitute.

I was so moved after reading some of Emily's writings that I connected with her. Over the phone we discussed sordid stories of internal bank discrimination and the overall issues of banking while being Black. No, I wasn't imagining that I was being treated unjustly. I was indeed being treated unjustly.

AMPLIFYING MY DISSATISFACTION

When I was denied my first refinance loan, it was before I married my CEO husband who runs a public company. For him, financing has never been an issue. He gets unsolicited offers daily for loans, credit cards, and mortgages. All the while, I don't get the same options or offers, and my assets are greater than his.

I decided, as my parents had taught me, that a closed mouth does not get fed. Just as my father had done, by putting pickets on banker's homes and local branches, I too would have to amplify my dissatisfaction. I started writing letters to the president of our local branch where my complaints got sent to special investigation. After waiting 3 months, the token minority bank staff person assigned to my case said that although she agreed with my assessment, there was nothing she could do. Next, I mailed Mellody Hobson, the African American woman who happens to be married to George Lucas, creator of *Star Wars*. Hobson joined the JPMorgan Chase board of directors in January 2018, and she was the first African American woman to hold this position. After reading of her decision to join based on JPMorgan Chase being a world-class institution and the largest bank in America, and that the bank was focused on financial literacy, I was moved to share my history. As Hobson is quoted as saying on the JPMorgan Chase website: "I think about how I can make the bank a stronger place. If the bank is diverse, we will be stronger." Perhaps my email did not make it up the chain because I never received a response. My father always taught me to go straight to the top, so my final letter went to the chairman himself, Jamie Dimon. The email I sent to office of the chairman is as follows:

Dear Mr. Dimon,

I wanted to bring your attention to a situation which has impacted my family financially. The brief synopsis of my complaint is yet another discriminatory example of loan bias.

I am a second-generation African American real estate investor in Seattle. I am a single fifty-five-year-old woman who works with my still active eighty-eight-year-old mother and now twenty-six-year-old third generation investing son.

My account balances with Chase are all north of seven figures. I completely reinvested hundreds of thousands of dollars back into buildings our family has owned for the past five decades, most with Chase loans. Each and every loan application and approval has been a battle. I requested a refinance of a triplex which Chase appraised at $1.3 million with an underlying balance of $450,000. I was only requesting 60% LTV to recoup some of the capital expenditures we had on renovations. Chase denied our loan and I requested an explanation as to why we were not considered for an exception. Please note, all my mortgages have been timely. I have never filed a bankruptcy and my properties are all in great condition. I even had to pay off a home in Scottsdale, Arizona, valued at $650,000, as I was not able to get a loan for this property, which is now free and clear.

The full correspondence of my complaint is detailed below. I feel our treatment was along the lines of Jimmy Kennedy.

I earnestly hope this situation can be explored and brought to light, so that the mistreatment of African American businesses can cease, and we can obtain the same opportunities to flourish as our white contemporaries.

I will await your response and I appreciate your time and consideration.

Sincerely,

Dana Frank

General Managing Partner

TD Frank Family Properties

My complaint was recycled back to the same special investigations department and was never resolved. I ended up removing my money from Chase and getting a refinance elsewhere.

PERSISTENCE PAYS

On March 9, 2016, the *Seattle Times* featured my mother and me in an article called "Persistence Pays for Black Family Buying Rentals in Seattle's CD since the 1950s." The article recounted our family history and reflected how the neighborhood and gentrification changed the landscape of our community, but how we prospered by staying put. We needed bank funding to continue to upgrade, renovate, and compete with the massive new construction led by firms who had access to bank financing. One Chase banker suggested we sell one of our buildings with equity if we needed cash, a suggestion ignorant of the double-whammy impact this would have on us of losing an asset and paying high capital gains.

By sharing our story publicly in the *Seattle Times,* we were able to connect with a banker named Jennifer Cherney, who researched our portfolio, saw the value, and invited us to lunch. My mother joked that Jennifer was not real because for 60 years of banking while Black, she had never had a banker cold call and offer lending at favorable rates and cash back refinance. It was a sad commentary considering the vast estate we had amassed.

If we have any hopes of long-term family wealth for minorities, investing is the only solution.

Like cops, not all bankers are bad bankers. Through the years, my mom and I have had the good fortune to encounter a few who believed in us and have worked to help us succeed, such as Cherney.

We must, as a community, hold banking institutions and appraisers accountable to their promises to create equity.

It's never too early to start the lessons. I so wish Daymond John's book, *Little Daymond Learns to Earn,* would have been available when I had nightly story hour with my children. Our collection included lessons from the Berenstain Bears (a family of Bears), Arthur (an Aardvark), and Junie B. Jones (a precocious adorable, blonde 6-year-old). I have such fond memories of those characters. However, our children need real stories of real people who look like us and lessons that we don't teach in school. Bravo to Daymond for the inspiration and outreach. We must give children the edge to get up and get on it.

GET UP AND GET ON IT!

- Research, reach out, and establish a relationship with your banker. This is key.

- Research opportunities like those listed in this chapter and pursue participation in them.

- When you feel you've been unjustly denied a loan, amplify your grievance. Write a letter to the bank manager, to the general manager, the CEO, and the chairman of the board. Write a letter to your local paper and television station. We must all be willing to stand up and make noise about what is unjust if we want change to be made.

- J.P. Morgan Chase, Bank of America and Wells Fargo are all commercial banks with over a trillion in domestic assets. There is money available to resource. Visit your local branches, credit unions, and lending institutions and establish relationships. Don't be intimidated to take your banker or lenders to lunch and learn what it will take to get you qualified.

- Amplify your requests. It's imperative as you build your financial future that you work with the right team of advisors, bankers, and circle. Let modern day athletes who are educated on financial literacy become the norm and not the exception. Invest in your future and educate others; however, eliminate all those who believe you should bankroll their lives off your labor.

- Contact your local bank chapters and inquire about these programs if you are a candidate.

- As you progress on your wealth and investment journey, be cautious of "shiny object syndrome." Certain investment opportunities may look appealing, such as the custom car business my father went into that was disastrous. Pick a lane and stay in it.

- Develop a solid business plan. Business students at your local universities can help you structure a strategic plan and numerous online free courses.

- Be a self-advocate, as my father proved to be, and remember, a closed mouth does not get fed.

5

HBIC
(Head Bitch in Charge)

Business is a man's world or so they say
Women work twice as hard, yet earn half the pay
Hey career girl, look at you, bringing home the bacon
Two incomes required for the lifestyle you're makin'
The body clock is tickin', it's time to have a baby
Excuse me, boss, is my job safe? He shrugs a maybe
Bank on yourself and find a way to invest
Time and appreciation mean equity on every wealth-building test
An entrepreneur builds life on her own terms
Working woman to CEO or president of your own firm.

—Dana Frank

Being a woman in business, or an HBIC, which is a "head bitch in charge," as I often say, requires setting aside preconceived notions and addressing the way others perceive us, which my father ensured I'd have plenty of practice doing.

"Name me one Black woman who has what I'm prepared to give you," he would often say to me. "Just one! Name one!"

"Oprah Winfrey is doing all right," I'd fire back, pleased with myself. At which point he'd scream at me to find examples not in the entertainment industry.

My father openly admitted to being a male chauvinist. I often joked with him that God must have a great sense of humor, considering that all his children turned out to be girls. He'd frequently make condescending remarks, trying to provoke a reaction from my sisters and me. Comments like, "Oh, it must be your time of the month," or "Don't let Bitchology get in the way of understanding what I'm trying to teach you," were all too common. Every day, we would wake up to newspaper clippings pasted on the kitchen cupboards, conveying messages that reinforced his perspective and diminished the validity of ours. These clippings covered a range of topics, from the importance of financial planning and avoiding inheritance taxes to Dear Abby columns on family conflicts. There were snippets about the economy, the rental market, and how businesses struggled with deficit spending during the recession. Often, he would add his own handwritten notes, like his holiday greeting, "Merry Christmas to YLIMAF." Puzzled, I asked him whom exactly he was referring to. Daddy's response was, "Come on now, don't be slow, that's from your mama's side. YLIMAF is *family* spelled backward, and that's how I feel dealing with all of you." He would then summon us for a family meeting, where he would berate us for spending time on what he deemed to be "fiddle-faddling." Getting manicures, going to the hair salon, my mom's modeling shows, or shopping were not activities that generated money, so he considered them trivial. My mother, sisters, and I developed a system to signal to one another when he was coming so we could quickly appear busy and avoid confrontation or blowouts.

He never succeeded in riling me up, as the saying goes, and I never bought into his belief that the weaker sex was female. I have come to operate like a non-stick pan. I do not allow other people's ignorance or envy of the lifestyle I have created affect my ability to operate.

I still marvel at the preconceived notions—about either my race or my sex or both—on display when mere strangers ask me how long I've been "manager" of this building or that property. I've come to enjoy the look of surprise on their faces when I respond that I own it. Often, they'll dig deeper, further reinforcing their ignorance, when they ask what my husband does for a living. When I share that we are in a commuter marriage and that the company over which I preside was formed by my parents more than 70 years ago, I can see they are even more baffled. While it may be true that I don't look the part, or act the part for that matter, due to my casual attire or the fact that my mother's genes have served me well and I don't look my age, time and again I know the looming question on their minds is, "How did she, a Black woman born in the 1960s, acquire, maintain, and grow a thriving property investment and rental management company?" We women in business need to be sure we speak up, we need to pay attention to how others around us are perceiving us, and we need to treat other women in business with respect. I'll come back to this one in a moment.

But first, we need more women to start, run, and grow their own businesses. The number of women-owned businesses has been steadily increasing over the years. In 2017, there were approximately 1.1 million women-owned businesses in the United States, comprising 20% of all employer firms, according to the US Census Bureau's 2019 Annual Business Survey (US Census Bureau, 2021).

However, despite this progress, women still face underrepresentation in various demographic groups. Most women-owned businesses tend to be small, with 90% of them having no employees, and more than half of women employers have only one to four employees (Williams, 2021).

A study commissioned by the Small Business Administration's Office of Advocacy reveals that women often operate smaller businesses in industries with lower growth potential. Specifically, women tend to cluster in retail, personal services, and professional services, with the "professional, scientific, and technical services" category being the most popular among women-employer firms, making up nearly 17% of them (Wright, 2022).

Interestingly, recent data suggests that Black female entrepreneurs are launching businesses at higher rates than White men. According to a report by *Harvard Business Review*, 17% of Black women in the United States are in the process of starting or running new businesses, compared to 10% of White women and 15% of White men (Kelley, Majbouri, and Randolph, 2021). However, there is a significant drop-off when it comes to Black female entrepreneurs running mature businesses, with only 3% continuing to do so. Obstacles such as limited access to capital and launching businesses in crowded marketplaces with lower margins contribute to this drop-off (Zalis, 2021).

These statistics highlight the importance of gaining access to seed capital for launching and investing in businesses. I can personally relate to this challenge, as my mother and I faced financial difficulties when we began our partnership in 1989. After my parents' divorce and property division, the properties we inherited were in disrepair due to a lack of property management by a court-ordered receivership. To upgrade the properties, raise the resident clientele, and increase rental income, we needed hundreds of thousands of dollars in liquid capital.

At that time, we had to make a crucial decision: either sell the properties at a discount or fight to rebuild. Selling would have provided some financial gain, but after paying capital gain taxes, our profits would have been temporary. Faced with this daunting task, we devised a strategic plan. I immersed myself in research, reading books and editorials and conducting online investigations on banking and lending. Through this process, I discovered the concept of a bank moratorium, which allows borrowers to temporarily stop making mortgage payments.

We set up a meeting with our local banker, where we shared our vision and intent to rebuild. By obtaining a bank moratorium for a year, we could utilize all our income toward refurbishing the properties. Up until then, we had always relied on refinancing to access cash. However, due to the properties' state of disrepair, an appraisal would not have generated enough value to secure the necessary funds. Once we successfully renovated the buildings, we were able to refinance and replenish our bank account.

During the recession of 1990, I made a tough decision that turned out to be one of my most profitable investments. I decided to refinance a 20-unit apartment building that I had not initially planned to encumber until it was time to finance my children's college education. Recessionary times often present great opportunities, and in this case, I found a 35-unit apartment building listed significantly below market value.

By refinancing the first building, I obtained the funds needed to purchase the new property, which has since proven to be a highly lucrative investment.

Maybe you're working on growing your business. Maybe you've not yet started your business but you're thinking about it. Maybe you're not sure you can. I'm here to tell you that it's unlikely there are any odds stacked against you that are impossible to overcome.

Just ask Rosemarie Francis.

RAGS TO RICHES WITH ROSEMARIE FRANCIS

It was beyond comprehension that the woman sitting across from me, radiating confidence and elegance with her captivating blue eyes and auburn highlights, had overcome the tumultuous and poverty-stricken past I'd read about to achieve remarkable success.

It felt like fate had brought Rosemarie Francis and I together as friends. We were both in the same stage of life—single, divorced, and mothers—and we shared common interests as real estate investors and writers. I'd just read her book, *The Better Life Book,* and learned she grew up in abject poverty outside Winnipeg, Manitoba, in a trailer lacking basic amenities and with an abusive alcoholic father.

I'd invited Rosemarie to meet for lunch, and she told me more about what drove her out of that life and into the one where she seemed on top of the world.

"I knew I wanted more out of life. I wanted a house with indoor plumbing and carpeting," she told me. "I wanted to wear nice clothes to work. I wanted to not worry about money."

She left home when she was 17 years old, graduated from high school and knew she would need a postsecondary education to achieve the goals she had set for herself. So, she worked a full-time job during the day and studied accounting at night. And this was the first step in Rosemarie significantly changing the trajectory of her life.

She made her first significant real estate investment when she was just 18 years old: a small two-bedroom, one-bath house, just 650 square feet, in Winnipeg. Using $2,000 her grandmother had left her when she passed and about $800 that she'd managed to scrape together for the down payment and other purchase costs, she bought the house for $26,000. The house needed a little TLC, and Rosemarie painted, replaced carpets, and after qualifying for a government grant, upgraded to energy-efficient doors and windows. All of this while she was making about $850 per month gross.

"The house looked quite cute once all of the work was done," Rosemarie said, putting down her fork and leaning back in her chair. "After 3 years, I sold the house for $43,000 and made more money in that one transaction than I did working full time for a year."

That was just the beginning, and now Rosemarie has accumulated an impressive portfolio of owned properties and wealth and recently—again overcoming resistance and odds—completed a deal that she says separated her from the pack.

"It was when I bought the dirt for an 83-unit development project. I had a few people that were quite negative on the deal. Despite that I worked through all the due diligence to mitigate the risk. I found a bank that was very supportive of a local female developer. I found a great general contractor that I trusted and had a great reputation."

It took Rosemarie's team 14 months to build a four-story, 84-unit apartment building. She personally inspected every unit, put upgraded finishings in, and is very proud of what she created. She even made the building pet-friendly despite property managers and others advising otherwise. Now pet-friendly is the standard in her community.

"I will never forget standing on a balcony of one of the units on the fourth floor watching move-in day. People were happy, the doggies were happy, and my heart was happy."

Rosemarie is so much more than a woman in business: she's a woman in the real estate investment business who overcame steep odds, found creative ways to start building her real estate portfolio and personal wealth, and she's cool, too.

Navigating Challenges as a Woman

In the real estate development world, Rosemarie often runs into men who think they are the smartest person in the room.

"I have certainly run into my share of men who have challenged me and discounted me simply because I am a woman," Rosemarie said. "I ran into this more when I was unknown and getting started in the development world. Now when it happens, I am very quick to advise the other person on how I expect our relationship to work and how I expect to be treated."

Rosemarie's experiences in this area mirror my own, unfortunately.

This is one of the reasons it's important to approach business decisions without letting emotions cloud judgment. Women often feel compelled to over-explain to avoid hurting someone's feelings. However, in business, there is no need for excuses or accepting them. It is possible to maintain compassion while also asserting oneself.

I learned this lesson early on when I had a plumber who consistently avoided providing a clear bill. After a month, he presented a tally that exceeded his initial estimate by tens of thousands of dollars. When I questioned him, he suggested buying the property from me and using his bill as a down payment. Although we reached a settlement, I vowed never to hire him again and realized the importance of being cautious and having everything in writing.

As your business grows and prospers, you may unfortunately experience changes in how friends and family perceive you and what they believe you owe them. We have encountered situations where family members rented from us and caused extensive damage to our apartments, straining our relationships. Friends and family might also feel entitled to loans that they never repay, expecting us to finance their dreams or projects. Establishing boundaries and making others understand your financial obligations can be a challenging balance. While I strongly support charitable endeavors and contribute my knowledge, time, and skills to the best of my abilities, it is essential for others to respect that my money is not theirs to claim.

HBICs OF THE FUTURE

When I asked Rosemarie to share some of the greatest setbacks she has encountered as an HBIC, I was not surprised that she was talking about how other women had treated her.

As a young woman working in a corporate environment, she says she ran into other women who had what she called "Queen Bee" syndrome. This is when they want to stay on top and will do whatever they can to discount or sabotage other women who may threaten them.

"I ran into this a lot as a young woman," Rosemarie said. "I never understood why these women would not just want to help other women."

There are plenty of sayings and quotes about how women should support other women in business and in life. We are not crabs in a barrel fighting and crawling over each other to reach the top. I take this message to heart. If I see an attractive woman, even if she is a stranger on an elevator, I will pay her a compliment. If someone is well prepared or does a quality job, I acknowledge it. I fervently believe the universe has plenty of goodness to go around, and when I see another woman getting busy, it inspires me to be more and do more. I'd like it to inspire you, too. Envy is evil. Call it Karma, your spiritual beliefs, or nature, you cannot grow, be successful, or attract what's good if you resent someone else's good fortune.

One of the ways Rosemarie works to make things better for the HBICs of the future is in how she consciously approaches raising her daughters.

"From an early age I have always believed that a person is always happier when they are contributing and feel like they are an integral part of the home functioning," she said. "My girls have always had to do chores around the house. They also know their responsibility is to get the best grades they can."

Her daughters all have summer jobs and that is where they get their spending money from. Rosemarie is also a big believer in sports for kids. It makes them realize that they have commitments and obligations to other people, and they are responsible for showing up every day and to be the best they can be.

Being an example for her daughters is one of Rosemarie's driving motivators. "I want my daughters to know how much I love them," she said. "I want them to be proud of what their mother accomplished. I want them to be able to build and add to what I have created." Like Rosemarie, one of my greatest joys is supporting other women and their minority-owned businesses. Two of my best friends growing up were Leslie and Laurie Coaston, African American twin sisters. They decided to open a soul food restaurant in Seattle. As they did their research, I traveled with them to New York, where we dined at Jezabel, which in 1983, when it opened, was a precursor of today's upscale soul food diners. The eclectic interior and dishes that warmed your heart and soul created a vision to be recreated in the Pacific Northwest. Although the twins did not have culinary degrees and had never operated a restaurant, they did their due diligence and for nearly 20 years, their restaurant, the Kingfish Café, became the dining destination for locals as well as celebrities like Gwyneth Paltrow when they came to town. I also did not have a background in the food industry; however, on overflow nights, I found myself lending a hand, bussing tables, and passing plates of their signature dishes from red beans and rice to catfish and polishing it off with their mammoth, mouth-watering red velvet cake desserts.

The twins found a niche and built a thriving business, which for more than two decades sustained their family and the next generation. Upon entering the establishment, visitors would see lifesize photos of the sisters' roots, including their father as a child on a porch in Alabama to their distant cousin, Langston Hughes. One of the chefs who worked at the Kingfish in the early days, Kristi Brown, went on to open Communion, becoming a Conde Naste Award winner as one of the 12 best new restaurants in the world.

That experience of watching these women succeed inspired me to support other entrepreneurs. To maintain the rich African American history of the Central District, we have supported the opening and reestablishment of several minority-owned businesses.

Everything I have done for the last three decades has been about building a legacy of multi-generational wealth for my family and the generations to come. But it goes beyond that to other communities: women in business, Black women, children.

"I would love to be remembered as a woman who broke down barriers and was able to be successful in a man's world but still be a feminine woman," Rosemarie said as we wrapped up our lunch together. "I hope that my story will inspire other women to believe in themselves to pursue their dreams."

I hope so too, Rosemarie. I hope so too.

GET UP AND GET ON IT!

- Know your shit! Be knowledgeable in all aspects of your business, whether it's understanding the cost of a new water heater installation or the price of painting a unit. Knowledge is power, and it empowers women to overcome gender biases.

- Practice speaking up. And pay attention to how others around you are perceiving you and treating you. Don't adopt their bias about your or your abilities.

- Treat other women in business with respect.

6

ALL IN A DAY'S WORK

Once a job is begun
Never leave until it's done
Be the labor great or small
Do it well or not at all
These wise words, my Papa Jones, a carpenter nailed
And this solid advice has never failed
It's all in a day's work. . .

—Dana Frank

For many, the thought of being a landlord is overwhelming. I am often asked how I can be bothered with the interrupting nuisance calls of being an owner and operator. The only way I can express this is to liken property ownership to parenthood. Yes, there will sleepless nights, especially during the child's infancy. There will be tough-love years where you must hold your offspring accountable and make sure they put in the work as you oversee and guide their efforts. And finally, as your child matures into adulthood, hopefully your investment in them pays off handsomely, and you realize you've produced a contributing member of society, of whom you are extremely proud.

As the mother of two adult children, I attest that just as I invested time in the highs and lows of rearing my offspring, the investment of owning real estate is as challenging and as rewarding as when I engage with my kids today. So, invest and give birth to your future!

Being your own boss and steward of a family legacy business like ours is a blessing with inherent challenges, along with freedom and autonomy when my program is running well; however, sometimes it seems my cell phone is an extension of my body. For the most part, my time is my own, but there are periods when I must work seven days a week. I have accepted this as a part of the cost of being my own boss. I must be on call if a hot water tank bursts. I must arrange to have cars towed when they are parked illegally. I act as a counselor when residents are experiencing hardship, be it in personal relationships or death in the family.

Could I hire someone to take care of some, many, or all of those tasks? Certainly. However, I believe the positive results in being a housing provider are best achieved when you self-manage. I also find that residents appreciate dealing with an owner rather than a manager who does not have the same vested interest in the property. Typically, property managers charge 5% to 10% of the gross rents. If you are willing to put in some effort, it is well worth saving the hefty management fee.

PRACTICALITIES OF THE JOB

My busiest time is the beginning of each month. Our rents are due on the first and considered delinquent if they haven't been paid by the third. I can hear you saying, "But nowadays, with electronic banking, isn't rent collection a seamless breeze?" No. On-time rent collection is important so that I can fulfill my obligations: all my mortgage payments include an escrow account for taxes and insurance, and this amount is deducted automatically each month on from my bank account. When rents aren't received on time, it puts my reputation at risk.

Prequalifying applicants is mandatory. Prior to meeting a potential tenant, I gather as much information as possible. I'll ask for their names and a contact number that I can reverse search for verification. I ask when they are looking to move. This saves time because often people are looking several months in advance, and our rentals generally rent within 20 days. I ask how many people will be occupying the space. (It's imperative to know the occupancy capacity limits in your state.) We have had a couple fill out an application, then multiple families move into the unit. The wear and tear on a unit, plus the added utility costs and noise, are factors. I inquire about pets. As a rule, we accept neutered cats, up to two. We do not take dogs in our larger complexes because of barking issues and dog poop cleanup. It is baffling what people consider pets, and over the years I have encountered pet rats, snakes, and even once a pet pig roaming freely in the apartments. I ask where they're employed or what their source of income is.

One of the first questions my father would ask when an applicant applied for a rental was if they "own a vacuum?" People would remark that it was a strange question, and my father would reply, "How are you going to keep my apartment clean if you don't own a vacuum?" When dealing with prospective tenants, there is so much more than what shows on an application.

Prequalifying saves time and the runaround for all parties. Not every lead is worthy, so the due diligence pays. Our rent requirements are listed in our advertisement. I have also discovered that if one property does not fit a need, I may have others in my inventory or upcoming to share.

I try to negotiate my leases to not run out in the months of November, December, or January because those are challenging rental seasons due to the holidays. We do a standard 1-year lease; however, I will occasionally offer shorter terms to avoid, for example, a November 30 move-out.

As a rule, our family does not require first, last, and a large deposit to move in. If a prospect has a good rental reference, paid rent timely, and is gainfully employed, we do not see the necessity to charge such massive move-in costs. We check an applicant's driver's license upon taking said application. Our criteria include employment history, pay stub, and references from previous rental history. We also require a three-to-one income-to-rent ratio to ensure the applicant can afford the rent. This means that if the rent is $2,000 per month, the combined gross income of tenants to qualify for the unit should be $6,000 per month. If the rent is going to be too steep for the tenant, there's a higher risk we'll have trouble collecting the rent from them at some point down the road. Even when we take all these precautions, still we encounter tenants who do not pay their rent on time.

NEW TENANTS AND TURNOVER

Today, we housing providers have all manner of tools at our disposal to try to attract leads (potential renters) to fill any vacancies. But my father had to work harder to find new tenants because he didn't have Craigslist or Zillow or Trulia or any other web-based social platforms.

So, we had to advertise in the *Seattle Times* and other periodicals or hang up Now Renting signs on the properties and at local shops. As part of our background check for applicants, we would call to verify landlord history and employment. He'd inspect the inside of an applicant's car and visit their residence. When asked about the odd and intrusive questions and inspections, Daddy's response was, "How will you keep my property up if you don't keep your current place clean?"

As a general practice, my father would also poach potential renters from open houses. The only resource for filling vacancies was the Wanted to Rent section in the *Seattle Times*. Waiting for the phone to ring was costly and time consuming.

On one afternoon, at an open house for a property we didn't own, Daddy overhead an Iranian man being denied an apartment. Mr. M and his wife and young son had relocated to Seattle after fleeing their home country when the Shah was overthrown. Mr. M, a skilled engineer, was without a job and had limited resources. Although he'd enjoyed an affluent lifestyle in Iran, to escape they had to leave it all behind.

Daddy followed a distraught Mr. M out to his car and told him to follow him to his new house. Mr. M was doubtful but desperate and followed my father to our residence as requested. He and his family moved into the illegal adjacent apartment that my father built for my sisters. Daddy bartered, and Mr. M drew up engineering plans to submit for a variance to legalize the unit in exchange for rent.

"Bastardizing" Your Properties

The key to winning in real estate apartment rentals obviously is making sure your income exceeds your expenses. This can be determined with your financing, interest rate, and potential market rate rent collections. My father believed in maximizing rental income by a process we called "bastardizing," which literally translates into changing something by adding new elements. The bastardized apartment would convert one-bedroom units into two, and two bedrooms into three, by carving out space in the living area. If a room has a window and closet and is roughly 10 by 12 feet, it's considered a bedroom. During the COVID-19 pandemic, when working from home became a reality for so many, these smaller third bedrooms translated into a bonus office space. Through the years, we have significantly increased revenue by instituting this practice. As micro units have become popular, residents do not seem to balk at the reduced living space. Housing costs have increased so much that single tenants are increasingly finding rents unaffordable. Creating that extra bedroom has solved an important issue and enabled more tenants to find roommates.

We have also implemented interior improvements, which can last for several rental turns. We no longer invest in laying carpets, which can stain and do not handle the wear and tear of traffic or pets. We now install only wood laminate floors, which are a clean alternative and when laid properly have a much longer longevity than carpet. We also have upgraded our kitchens with granite counters and LED lighting, which last for extended periods.

We use a standard off-white paint across the board on all units, so touchup is easy. Utilizing the same nuts and bolts on all the rentals makes it possible to literally move someone out on the 31st and have a unit turned for a new resident within 24 to 48 hours, thus without a loss of revenue.

HIRING MAINTENANCE WORKERS

So, you want to be a landlord? Finding quality help can be a challenge. My father's solution was to take tenants, or any able-bodied person willing to work, and put them to work.

Daddy sat at his cluttered office desk. The crew that he called his "hired handicapped" were tenants who had become maintenance men. Mac, Mr. Florence, and Freddie all filed in the office at 8:10 a.m. Monday morning.

"Well, good afternoon," Daddy said sarcastically, seeing that he had been up and at it since five that morning. "Freddie, go to Spring Street and detail that one-bedroom." Freddie, a single father in his late 20s, was mild-mannered and eager to please.

"Spring Street," Freddie repeated.

Ignoring Freddie, Daddy turned to the listless Mr. Florence who, as usual, looked fatigued. The 67-year-old had sullen eyes and an expressionless face. "Mr. Florence, wake up!" Daddy screamed, startling the elder soul. "You and Mac are gonna be painting at 27th and Cherry. Go in the garage; there's some oyster-white paint. Use semi-gloss throughout the place. Now, the lady moving in is on a Section 8 housing voucher and her inspection is Wednesday. You know the rules. No chipped paint or it won't pass inspection, and I won't get paid."

Daddy returned to his notes. His crew stood looking at him as if waiting for more instructions. "Get up and get on it! I ain't talkin' Swahili," my father barked.

The workmen headed out in our company's truck, its license plate hanging precariously over the tail pipe.

I have found when hiring employees, you must understand their *why*. For the past 30-plus years, I have had a maintenance foreman, Eddie, who I sometimes joke is my husband from the waist up because we spend so much time together. Eddie's *why* is answered because he is a family man, a husband, father, and grandfather, and he works to support and enjoy those he loves and his life. Eddie truly is a part of the family. We have also ensured his future security with retirement plans. If you find a committed employee who supports your efforts, then I believe they should be rewarded.

And I have learned to embrace the fact that some who start out as maintenance workers may be destined for greater things.

Shahab Khademi is one such example. Born and raised in Tehran, Shahab came to the United States to pursue an engineering education at Seattle University. That's where he met my sister, who was studying business and journalism. It was a cultural exchange on a micro level, with my sister learning to appreciate and create dishes like Salad Olivieh, a Persian potato salad, and Shahab gaining exposure and insights into the real estate investment business. When my sister suggested he stay in the United States after graduation and work for my father instead of moving to Canada where his family had settled, he agreed, while admitting he had never done manual labor.

So, my father assigned him the task of cleaning a vacant unit and working alongside two men hired to hang wallpaper. He watched the installation process, and when the two contractors left without finishing the job, Shahab took it upon himself to complete the project. He surprised everyone, including my father, with his seamless workmanship.

This proved to be a turning point for Shahab. After graduation, and under the guidance of my father, Shahab teamed up with my sister and another friend for their first investment—a five-unit apartment complex. From that moment on, Shahab's life took a new direction. He modeled his career after the lessons he learned from my father and dedicated himself to acquiring, operating, and managing multifamily apartment buildings.

Today, at the age of 72, Shahab's hard work and perseverance have paid off. He has achieved great success in the real estate industry. He owns a beautiful home overlooking Lake Washington as well as a second home in Scottsdale, Arizona. As we sat together in his rose-filled garden sipping wine, Shahab shared that my father became his best friend and played a pivotal role in changing the path of his life. He produced the job logbook he's been hanging onto for the past 40 years, which details long, tedious 10-hour days, for which my father paid him $4 per hour. This is what instilled in him a drive and understanding that he had a choice: he could work for someone else or build his own dream.

His success has not only benefited him but also his wife and adult daughter, who have joined him in the family business, ensuring generational wealth and a lasting legacy.

Shahab's story serves as an inspiration for the power of mentorship, cultural exchange, and seizing opportunities. But it is also all in a day's work, a reminder that you never know exactly how you will impact and influence those you hire in your real estate investment business.

FALLING IN LOVE WITH YOUR PROPERTIES

I admit I have failed at the one rule every real estate investor will tell you and that is not to fall in love with your property. Real estate code is to fall in love with the numbers, and when you have depreciated the property and no longer reap the benefits from writeoffs, or you experience negative cash flow, you should sell and move on to the next project.

A successful investor and his wife who are friends of mine are much better at putting this into practice than I am. They've given me permission to share these details but asked me not include their real names, so I'm calling them Bill and Diane.

Bill and Diane view real estate as an asset and do not become emotionally attached to any of their properties. This mindset allows for more objective decision-making and enables them to make strategic moves for long-term wealth creation. They've also thoroughly embraced a mobile lifestyle, frequently moving between properties under renovation. In fact, in a 32-year marriage they have moved 40 times! Their willingness to live in houses while they are being improved has allowed them to oversee the renovation process closely, maximize their investment potential, without getting attached. Once the work is done, they move on.

As hard as I try, I can't do that. I treat my buildings like they are an extension of my family. I have pride of ownership, and I care about their well-being. I want them healthy from the inside out, with updated plumbing, electrical, leak-free roofs, and for the interiors to be welcoming, clean, and appealing. I drive by our different locations and inspect almost daily. I keep rubber gloves and trash bags in my trunk, and if there is trash on the ground,

I do a pickup. I inspect to make sure hallway light bulbs have not burned out. I greet my residents and respond to their repair requests in a timely fashion. Listing vacancies, showing prospective tenants' units, running background checks, signing leases, doing walk-throughs on move-ins and move-outs, paying the mortgages, utility bills, expenses, landscaping and running a maintenance crew, seasonal testing of swimming pool water in the buildings that have one—all are part of my daily activities. There was construction that lasted a year adjacent to one of our buildings, and as a sign of our appreciation for the residents' inconvenience, we gave them all Amazon gift cards. Happy residents make happy landlords.

But what to do with residents who have absolutely no regard for your property? It happens. Contemplate if you will for a moment your most prized possession. Is it your home? Your car? A family heirloom? A new rug? Or perhaps it's a special outfit that you loaned out. Now imagine that when your prized possession is returned to you, it is destroyed and no longer recognizable. When this happens to me, I get a hollow feeling in the pit of my stomach.

That's what I feel when I enter a unit filled with cigarette smoke or with damaged walls, soiled appliances, or animal destruction. Once, we rented to a resident who snuck in nine un-neutered cats. The new carpeting on the floor had to be removed, the wood underneath sanded and, in some places, replaced to combat the smell of cat urine. The tenant was a grown woman with a responsible job. She did not look like a crazy cat lady. However, what I have come to accept is that neither age, nor income, nor credit score, nor ethnicity, nor anything else can predict how someone will treat your property.

When each of my children elected to move into student housing at their respective universities, it broke my heart to see them leave the clean confines of the home life we had created. How could they choose to live among 85 strangers in the chaos, clutter, and often human waste left over from a night of a fellow student resident getting over-served at the pub? Even though I tried to feign indifference, I could not hide the horror from my expression. My son went to school in our home state, so I pleaded, "You can still be a part of this community. But you don't have to sleep here! Your room is ready for you at home. It's only a 15-minute drive away."

The thought of having my children leave the nest was tough enough. However, I truly couldn't imagine them sleeping in such squalid conditions. In frat after frat, dorm after dorm, who were these young adults? Didn't they ever have to do chores at home? Who can go to bed with a sink overflowing with dirty dishes? How can one function without basic household necessities such as Windex? Was a broom only an accessory at Halloween?

These same young adults who graduate with impressive degrees are the ones who 4 years later come calling for an apartment. They have mastered the sciences, arts, communications, and business; however, they never learned Housekeeping 101. These same students are the ones I hand over the keys to the pristine apartments I have detailed to perfection. I know they're pristine because I do a walk-through inspection with each new tenant before they move in. I go through my list proudly:

- Walls: painted.
- Floors: new with laminate throughout.
- Countertops: granite clean.

- Stove: I open the door to show the inside gleaming.
- Refrigerator: clean, with an open box of baking soda on the top shelf at the back.

I go through every nook and cranny searching and noting the slightest defect. My maintenance and cleaning teams are impeccable. The window seals are scrubbed. The chrome faucets sparkle on the tub, sink, and kitchen fixtures. The windows are washed and so transparent one could mistake them for being open. I was raised cleaning these same interiors and so it is a part of my DNA to make sure the result is a unit I could personally sleep in.

Often, as a housing provider, I feel our work has been in vain. The new resident gleefully signs the lease and acknowledges the spic-and-span interior on the walk-through, and 1 year later, I often find myself horrified at the destruction they have caused in just 365 days.

Mr. W and His Mental Illness

In 1999, my mother and I purchased the Genesee Park Apartments. At the time, the location was considered a transitional neighborhood. The zip code of 98118 in Southeast Seattle is the one of the most diverse in the United States. We saw the desirability: the Sound Transit Light Rail line offering easy access to the University of Washington and SeaTac Airport. A PCC Market, Starbucks, farmer's market, and renovations underway in properties nearby proved the community was on the rise. To acquire the property, we refinanced one of our other 20-unit buildings to generate the down payment.

Prior to our purchase, in its heyday, the building was a crown jewel with an indoor swimming pool, elevator, balconies, and a mix of spacious one- and two-bedrooms. The two-bedroom, two-bathroom apartment homes had nearly 2,000 square feet of living space. The previous owner had allowed the property to deteriorate, and now there was old carpet, outdated interiors, and a backlog of deferred maintenance. These poor conditions are called "value add" for a purchaser willing to put in the time, effort, and money to increase the property's worth. In addition to cosmetic upgrades, this building needed a new roof, exterior paint, and parking lot replacement. The owner and the elderly residents had an agreement: don't ask for repairs, and the rent would remain below market.

When Mom and I took ownership, we secured financing and immediately commenced upgrading the building and units to restore her to her prime. An elderly man I'll call Mr. W had lived in one of the two-bedroom units for 25 years. He would never allow us access to his unit and claimed all was well behind the door of his suite. When we replaced the windows in the entire building, he refused to let the contractors inside, and they had to do the installation from the exterior. Because of his history of loyal tenancy, we respected his desired privacy. One chilly November, Mr. W had not paid his rent, and it was already mid-month. Records showed us he was always an early payer, and every month he left his check in the manager's slot before any of the other residents. His tardiness alarmed me, so I knocked at his door. Without opening the door, I heard a weak voice saying he had the rent; he just needed a few days to get to the bank.

Every couple of days for a week I went back. Each time, Mr. W sounded more lethargic. Finally, concerned about his welfare, I called the fire department, and a crew came and kicked the door in. (Mr. W had changed the locks, which is against code. Landlords must have a master key to access a unit in the case of fire or other emergencies.)

Mr. W's apartment

Once the door was kicked in, the firemen, my mother, and my crew stood aghast at the scene before us. It was the worst case of hoarding I could imagine. Every square foot of the two-bedroom unit was filled floor to ceiling with trash. And Mr. W was buried in the hall in the middle of it. There were newspapers dating back 30 years, old car tires, books, records, pots full of his feces, bottles of his urine, broken furniture, old uniforms, axes, and hoses. The plumbing had long ceased to operate in the apartment; the kitchen appliances were inoperable and inaccessible as they too were besieged with trash.

Mr. W was taken to the hospital where he pleaded with us not to remove any items. We agreed to wait until his release. Once he was home, and we began to work with him to clean out his unit, it proved a painstaking process because Mr. W could not bring himself to part with anything. Not even the wads of used toilet paper. We helped Mr. W get hospitalized for treatment of his mental illness. Unfortunately, Mr. W died before he could return to his apartment. It is not how we would choose to remove a problematic tenant, of course, but I share this story to demonstrate the range of experiences you may find yourself dealing with as a housing provider.

Fortunately, contrary to popular belief, not all landlord and tenant relations are adversarial. We have several residents with whom we've had extremely long-term relationships. There have been families who resided in our properties for 10, 20, and as long as 50 years. We have watched as they have raised their children and become grandparents. Some have married, and we have attended their celebrations. Some have become our computer technician, rental agent, or joined our maintenance crew. Others have moved away and come back.

One young single mother had escaped an abusive husband. She and her parents had been struck by tragedy when her sister was murdered by the sister's husband. She was struggling financially without any family support, and she and her toddler daughter were living in their car. The year was 2003 when she and her daughter moved into one of our buildings. She got a job at a local grocery store and worked her way up into management. She raised her daughter who graduated with honors, and 19 years later, they are still residing in the same apartment. The rent is not nearly at market rate. However, the payoff of being a part of helping change someone's future is priceless.

Understanding that the business of being a landlord is not just running a building, it is ensuring the enjoyment, entitlement, and safety of one's home. It is the most rewarding feeling when someone walks in and falls in love with a space.

GET UP AND GET ON IT!

- In addition to managing a work crew with detailed property inspections, neighborhood analysis for rent pricing and trends, advertising, marketing, and accounting, you will need a comprehensive management plan.

- As you move toward becoming a real estate investor and housing provider, remember to approach your properties a little like a parent: the hard work you put into developing them will pay off later.

- Be sure to develop a thorough prequalification process that will help set you up to find the right tenants and mitigate the risks associated with the problem ones.

- Perform all background, reference, and credit checks on potential applicants.

- Check your property daily or often.

- Invest in your property as you would your own child. I believe what you put into your buildings in upkeep, maintenance, repairs, and proper response to tenant issues will be magnified in your pro forma and bottom line.

- Every business gets work fatigue. Be ready to give up some of your weekends when vacancies mount. In real estate, you must be willing to commit to the grind that often comes with emergency late-night calls and weekend shifts.

7

RENT AND EVICTIONS

Rent is due and the money's been spent

Frivolous expenditures now to lament

Landlord says she's got mortgages, taxes, and utilities to pay

Eviction Notice Served, nothing left to say

The housing provider is to blame

When it's the tenant who failed to make the time frame

Those four walls come with a cost

If the bank forecloses, all will be lost

Rent is due, so pay on time

Squatting is stealing, and that's a crime

Keep your credit good and your record clean

One day you will be a homeowner and know what I mean

— Dana Frank

December is notoriously the worst month for collections. Residents fabricate the most imaginative tales of why they cannot pay, when the rent has been spent on the celebratory season:

> "My baby flushed the rent check down the toilet. I'm waiting for the government to reissue it."

> "My woman, she needed an abortion."

> "My car broke down, and I had to use the rent money to get a new engine."

As frustrating as it is having nonpayers occupy your property and enjoy the benefits of warm shelter that, as a housing provider, you must provide—it is the law. I'll talk more about the law and legal issues shortly, but the sole recourse a landlord has is to file an Unlawful Detainer Action. An eviction, or Unlawful Detainer, is a legal process a landlord must follow to restore the property to the owner's possession. Actions such as changing the locks, removing a tenant's belongings, or disconnecting utilities are strictly prohibited.

No Rent? No Door

You know by now that my father was not one to wait for the law. There was one resident who ghosted us every month. One December, we continued to try to reach the resident and each day when we drove up to his home on 22nd Avenue, the curtains were drawn, and there was no sight of any activity. We had served him with what was the law back then, a 3-day notice to pay or vacate. The courts were backlogged; apparently, other landlords were dealing with the same issues, so we could not get a hearing until well into the new year.

Daddy wasn't having it. He knew the tenant had a job because we had verified his employment when he moved in. However, his rent had not once been paid on time since he moved in.

The inclement Seattle weather was pouring when my father arrived at our lead maintenance foreman's apartment at a little after 4:00 a.m. Ken stumbled toward the Dodge pickup, dribbling his coffee. With a cigarette hanging from his mouth, Ken held on to his mug and searched his ski jacket for matches. The lighter in the truck was missing. He found a rubber band and tied his long hair back into a ponytail.

Ken looked at his watch. "It's not yet five. I thought you were gonna have me finish the remodel on Eighteenth Street this morning."

"Yeah, son. What we must do will just take a minute. Then I'll send you on to Eighteenth to meet the rest of the crew."

They pulled up in front of the small three-bedroom, two-bath bungalow, painted yellow with black trim, on Twenty-second Avenue. The drapes were all drawn closed.

Ken opened the truck door. "Problem here, boss?" He asked.

Daddy nodded. "Yeah, there's a problem here all right. These suckers bounced their rent again. I need you to go up there and remove the front door. Take your master key and open it, then just remove the hinges, and stick it in the back of the pickup."

"What if they're in there?" Ken stood as rain pellets increased in size and fury. "They must be asleep now."

"All the better. Maybe this cold weather will wake their asses up to reality. Give 'em incentive to pay on time. They're playing me for a fool."

Ken reached the front porch with his master key and screwdriver in hand. "What should I say if they come to the door?"

"Tell them the door needs repair," Daddy snickered. "When they pay their rent, we'll have the money to replace it."

Ken came back to the pickup and put the black solid-core door in the back. The tenants had not awakened.

Twenty minutes later, my father breezed into his home office. My mother stood in her bathrobe holding the phone. She pushed the large red flashing hold button.

"Gerald, this is your tenant from Twenty-second on the line. He said his front door is missing."

"Aw, to hell with them," my father flagged his hand in a shunning motion. He pushed the speaker button. Leaning on the desk, he spoke loudly into the microphone. "Good morning, Gerald Frank here."

"Man, I just got up, and my front door is missing!" the tenant said.

"Now ain't that a coincidence?" My father chuckled. "Seems your rent is missing too."

"Man, you can't do that," the tenant screamed. "I'm calling the police."

"Don't threaten me. Go ahead and call the police. You'll look pretty stupid reporting a missing front door. I'm sure that will be right up there with all other patrol-duty emergencies. Just pay me my damn rent. And this time in cash. I know you're getting your paycheck. So, give me mine, and then you'll get your door back."

Now, obviously my father's tactics would not pass muster today. But he resorted to them when he felt he had no other choice. Some segments of renters are just deadbeat and don't like to pay.

Nobody is interested in protecting and growing your money more than you. If you are going to be a Fire Starter, owner, and operator, don't accept excuses and don't give them.

Terminating Tenancy with Cause

Seattle's Just Cause Eviction Ordinance prevents arbitrary evictions of tenants. It requires a housing provider to give a legal reason or just cause if they wish to terminate a tenant's lease. Per the Seattle *Renter's Handbook* (2022), you cannot terminate a tenant's month-to-month rental agreement unless the circumstances fit into one of these categories:

- Late rent. You receive a 14-day notice to pay or vacate and fail to comply.
- Habitual failure to pay rent on time. You receive four or more 12-day pay-or-vacate notices in the most recent 12-month period for late rent.
- Violation of your agreement. You issue to a tenant a 10-day notice to comply with the rules of their rental agreement or vacate and they fail to comply.
- Habitual failure to comply with their rental agreement. You have issued the tenant three or more 10-day notices to comply or vacate in the most recent 12-month period for failure to comply with the rules of the rental agreement.
- You or a member of your immediate family needs to move into a unit occupied by a tenant. This requires a 90-day notice and only applies to single-family dwelling units. You cannot use this as a reason to end a rental agreement if the tenant's unit is in an apartment, condo, townhouse, duplex, or triplex.
- You want to sell the unit you are renting to a tenant. This requires a 90-day notice and only applies to single-family dwelling units.

- Your tenant's occupancy of a unit depends on being employed *on the property* and you have terminated their employment. This would typically apply to property managers who live on site.

- You rent a portion of your own home or an accessory dwelling unit to your own home and no longer wish to share it with your tenant.

- You want to substantially remodel the unit or building where your tenant(s) live, displacing them permanently. This requires you to apply for a relocation license, which is approximately a 6-month process. The license requirements include giving the tenant(s) an information package and paying them relocation assistance if their rent is at or below 50% of the median income for the area.

- You want to demolish the property where your tenant lives or change the use to nonresidential. This requires a relocation license, the same as displacement from a substantial remodel.

- You want to convert your tenant's unit to a condo or a co-op, which requires its own procedure under Condominium and Co-operative Conversion Ordinance.

- You receive a notice of violation for an unauthorized housing unit, commonly called an illegal unit, and you must discontinue renting it. In this circumstance, you must pay to the tenant relocation assistance of either $2,000 or the equivalent of 2 months' rent prior to move-out.

- You are issued an emergency order to vacate and close your tenant's unit due to hazardous conditions. The notice requirement depends on the specific circumstances of the emergency but is a short period. Your tenant may get relocation assistance if the emergency condition is found to be your responsibility. Relocation assistance is adjusted for cost of living each year.

- You issue your tenant a 3-day notice to quit engaging in criminal activity on the property. You must specify the crime and facts supporting the allegation in the notice of termination.

You can see that once someone occupies your property, terminating the relationship is a process like getting a divorce. Harder, perhaps. You battle out your differences in court where a judge decides, and your financial assets are on the line. The process can be costly, time consuming, and honestly infuriating. But what about situations which don't fit into traditional just-cause reasons? I had such a circumstance.

Too Much for a Cat

For more than 2 weeks, each morning, the walls and carpet in the common stairwell of one of our 35-unit apartment buildings were saturated with urine.

The culprit could not be a cat. The amount of urine deposited into the stairwell would be too much for any feline. We assumed someone had snuck in a dog. Every day, residents of the complex complained. No one could explain how each morning the urine was redeposited after we sanitized daily with bleach. We were at our wit's end, when finally, we installed hidden cameras in the stairwell.

And that's how we discovered the perpetrator. At 5:45 a.m., the footage showed one of our residents walking down the stairs, dropping his pants, and spraying the walls as if his genitals were a fire hose. Clearly his bladder was full as he showered the walls, carpets, exit doors, and banister. When he was finished relieving himself, he got dressed, put his backpack on, and left.

We waited outside the door to his unit for him to get home from work, where he invited us inside. At first, he denied that he was causing the nuisance until we showed him the video footage. He and his new wife had recently moved in. They appeared to be ideal candidates for our renovated and spacious one-bedroom in the desirable neighborhood. They had easily passed the background screening with credit scores in the high 700s. There were no outstanding collections, evictions, or red flags. The couple was gainfully employed, each of them with a good position in a large and well-known corporation. The first month's rent and deposit had been paid with no issues before they moved in.

My mother and I stood in shock as he finally admitted to suffering with urolagnia, a condition where individuals get sexual stimulation at the smell of urine. Was he kidding? I had never heard of such a thing. He started using our stairwell because he was newly married and therefore could no longer sleep with his urine-soaked underwear. He didn't want his wife to know.

There are some images which will forever be imprinted in my memory, and one is of my mother at an age when most are long retired, with her manicured, orange-polished nails, as she pointed at the tenant and said, "When can you get the fuck out?"

We had confronted him on a Friday evening. The resident and his new bride had vacated the unit by the next day.

There is a rule in real estate investing that says, location, location, location. The same rule should apply with your resident profile: application, application, application. As evidenced by the previous story, you cannot judge a book by its cover or a tenant by their credit score.

THE EVICTION THAT COULDN'T WAIT FOR THE LAW

Neighbors had informed us that although the tenants had been evicted from the unit, they had managed to break a window and regain access to the apartment. In addition to the original tenants who were evicted, there were many other occupants who all appeared to be using drugs, based on the paraphernalia and constant traffic.

By the time we reached the unit, the door was shut, and all the blinds were closed. Daddy put his fingers to his lips and motioned for me to stand back and be quiet. He turned his master key quickly in the lock and flung the door open. "What the fuck are you doing in my property?" he roared.

The rail-thin man with coke-bottle glasses jumped off the couch. The unit was in complete disarray and full of trash from the families living in the 600-square-foot one-bedroom apartment. Burned-up bent spoons, residual heroin powder, cigarette butts, and marijuana blunts littered the coffee table.

Even though the apartment was crowded, these people were enjoying the shelter, heat, running water, and drugs to share.

"The Eviction That Couldn't Wait for the Law" was the headline the *Seattle Times* newspaper ran, featuring a full-page photo of my father hurling a tenant's belongings into a courtyard. The newspaper story said my father was fed up with waiting on the sheriff.

"Sometimes you have to be a vigilante and take the law into your own hands. These tenants were a menace to my community," the paper quoted my father saying. They called him "the controversial landlord" who personally removes those illegally occupying his property. Daddy always said if he had to sit back and wait for help from the City of Seattle, his property could be burned to the ground before they'd send anyone to help. "There were other tenants living around this unit. It's my responsibility to protect the lives of the other residents as well as their children," my father said in the story.

I do not subscribe to my father's tactics, of course, but I have learned to ward off problems early as they arise. Some residents just don't like to pay.

For this reason, if you are a housing provider, you must know the laws and utilize all tools to protect your asset prior to turning it over.

GET UP AND GET ON IT

- KYS: know your shit. Read up on the rent and eviction laws in your city and state and be sure you know your rights.

- Structure your own financial obligations so that you have a bit of flexibility to absorb a portion of your rent receipts not being paid on time.

- Be sure you are setting and communicating your late-payment and nonpayment policies with prospective tenants.

- Document each tenant's rent payment: day, time, method of payment. You will need to be able to review the habits and history.

8

IT'S THE LAW

There was a time when I couldn't marry my white husband, the law said so

It is said love is blind, didn't Plessy v Ferguson know?

Couldn't marry the same sex

While 50 percent of matrimonies end with an ex

Marijuana was illegal, how many sat incarcerated for selling?

Now billions are being made, retailers' profits are compelling

Couldn't rent out space in your home, until Airbnb

Mother-in-law apartments were not approved in the old decree

My body, my right

Speak up and fight

Rules and regulations, they called them the law

While we wait on the world to change, I reckon many are a flaw

—Dana Frank

Seattle imposes mandated limits on how often we can increase rents, and it seems like variations of attempted rent control are constantly on the agenda. Lawsuits are on the uptick with complaints from residents with a criminal history and poor credit that they're unjustly being denied tenancy. Laws are increasingly taking away a landlord's rights to control their own assets. This has discouraged many landlords from staying in the business or for others to become landlords.

What do you do when trying to make sense of the unreasonable? As I've covered in these chapters, our family business began when segregation was still the law. Interracial marriages won a victory with Loving Day, June 12, 1967. Black families were not allowed to join the Seattle Tennis Club, of which I am now a member. Same-sex marriages were against the law until February 2004. Marijuana became decriminalized in 1996, when California became the first state to legalize medical cannabis. The point is that laws change. And in the case of many of the laws surrounding property rental in Washington state, my view is many of them just don't make sense.

The pendulum has swung heavily in favor of the tenant. There needs to be an open dialogue between policymakers and housing providers about the burden of restrictions on whom housing providers must rent to. The Fair Housing Ordinance, for example, aims to address bias and barriers for people with criminal backgrounds who are attempting to secure rental housing. Of course, it is important that we help those who have paid their debts to society and are working hard on rehabilitation. We must also recognize that in some cases we put the safety of other residents at risk if the renter is a repeat or habitual offender and treatment or counseling has not helped.

We once had a repeat offender in one of our properties who assaulted a young teenager visiting the building. We were able to evict him. However, with the moratorium on evictions imposed during the pandemic, today we would not have that option.

THE DCLU VERSUS GERALD FRANK

During my father's lifetime, Airbnb didn't yet exist. The practices driving Airbnb's profits today were in fact illegal then. Since he made his first purchase, Daddy had been dividing rental units and creating mother-in-law apartments to generate revenue. We constantly found ourselves in a courtroom battling it out with the Department of Construction and Land Use (DCLU), which governs property usage. The DCLU issues permits, enforces code compliance, design review, zoning, and maintains measures to ensure the city's structure and safety of property.

Daddy believed it should be his right to add structures without waiting for permits—because they took too long to get approved. He didn't abide by their laws not to add additional levels to property, which might have an adverse impact on his neighbor's views. He did not agree with their zoning codes disallowing single-family residences to be operated as multi-family usage. If a single-family home could be transformed into a duplex or triplex, my father knew the income would triple.

"Daddy, you know the DCLU is always after you. This place is zoned for single family, and you've got three other families living around us."

He reached out and touched my knee. "But it's all a game. Explain to me how I was successful in beating them suckers at it. It's important. If something happens to me, you gotta know the game."

I moaned and peeked at the clock on the kitchen stove. "The law says up to nine unrelated people can live under the same roof, if there is only one stove. So, you moved the ranges out of the units next door when the DCLU came to inspect."

"Ah baby, it's much deeper than that. Go on, explain how I was able to get the jury to come in with such a large settlement."

The day of court, he wore chocolate-brown corduroy pants, a beige wool sweater, left his toupee at home, and carried a cane. I was seated in the courtroom with my mother and sister, Robin. Robin had done a fine job. She had been the first to testify. I had been terrified that I too would be called to take the stand. After Daddy entered the witness box, his attorney asked him to explain to the court why he had built the additional units onto his house.

"There is a disintegration of the Black family. Most Black children don't know who their fathers are. This is why there are drugs and gangs popping up in all major metropolitan areas. I created this housing for my children so that we could maintain our family unit while still giving my daughters the privacy and safety they deserve as young adult women. Most mansions have guest houses. They used to serve as the maid's quarters. The modern-day term is carriage house, but call them what you want, they're in every wealthy neighborhood. If I was a White man living in exclusive neighborhoods like Medina or Madison Park, I would never be subjected to this bureaucratic harassment."

On cross-examination, the attorney for the DCLU brought in copies of telephone directories showing the names of Mr. M and another resident at our address. Daddy didn't miss a beat as he lied that these former tenant names were names of his daughters' boyfriends who had phone lines at the house. He continued that he had a heart condition and said the situation was particularly stressful and had required his doctor to increase his medication.

The jury deliberated for 2 days and came back with an award in Daddy's favor. He received a substantial settlement.

I checked the clock. "What can I say? You just outsmarted them."

THE REVERSE-REVERSE

My father called his methods for dealing with blatant racism "the reverse-reverse," where he had to shed light on injustice through unconventional actions.

"Well, you said it was urgent," Ken replied dryly. He wiped the crusty sleep from his eyes. Daddy had first arrived at Ken's 500-square-foot unit at 5 a.m., and Ken was still dreaming when he heard the familiar bellow through the door urging him to get up. But Ken dozed off again. At 6:30 a.m., Daddy returned. When Ken did not answer, my father used his master key and let himself in.

At 8:43 a.m., Ken, recovering from the previous night's drinking, sped down the hill in his dented blue Datsun. Although he had begun the morning without the benefit of water touching his body, he tried to look alert. Ken was only 22, but he was the most skilled of our employees. He was the sole White guy on our team, but Daddy still called him "my number-one son." Ken had joined the team after relocating from Denver with his Afghan dog. He was a free-spirited alcoholic hippie with impressive carpentry skills.

Ken swept his ponytail to his back in an anxious gesture. He took a seat and wiped his eyes, then he set the coffee cup down, spilling some of the heavy cream and sugar he had added. "Sorry I'm late, boss," he said.

Ken watched as my father scattered the layers of papers around his desk. Somewhere under the rent checks, legal pads, message books, a receipt ledger, applications, and complaint letters from tenants, Daddy found a pad of paper and started a list.

"Ken, damn, why can't you get your ass up in the morning? Half the day is gone."

Ken shrugged and took the admonishment.

"Well, son, I had to get you up early." Daddy looked at the clock hanging next to the bookshelf. "Actually, it's a little late now for what I had in mind. You're gonna have to do it either late tonight, I'm talking close to midnight, or I can get your ass up at four or five in the morning."

"Okay, so what's up?"

Daddy leaned back in his chair. The rest of his methadone maintenance crew would arrive any minute.

"It's the property out there on Queen Anne."

"The duplex you just bought?"

"Yep, the one we just added the two extra illegal units to making it a fourplex. I had to bring in more revenue to cover the mortgage. The neighbors are upset because they didn't want the Black families moving in next to them. They threatened me to move them out or to suffer the consequences and when I refused, they called the fucking Department of Construction and Land Use."

Daddy passed Ken the citation from the city.

"Oh, shit," Ken said, glancing at the document. "After your last victory and getting that big settlement, you know they'll be on you."

"Son, they're gonna be on me like white on rice. So, as usual, I gotta come from a position of strength. Here's my plan." He leaned forward in his chair and faced Ken. "You gotta go out there and spray-paint across the garage in the biggest, blackest letters: Blacks Get Out!"

Sign painted on our property on Queen Anne Street

"What?!" Ken tossed his head back, laughing. "Come again? You want me to spray-paint that on the new white automatic garage doors we just installed?"

"You heard me right, son. I know those racist bigots won't be able to stand the heat. I'm the only Black man that owns something on that block. Once I get the community to sign petitions saying that I'm being treated unjustly, I can get the city off my back. It's that simple." Daddy smiled.

Ken shook his head in disbelief and looked my way for support. I could offer none.

"Boss, couldn't you go to jail for. . .I dunno?"

"That's why you gotta be slick. Don't let nobody see you and don't tell a soul."

"You really think that will work?"

"Son, I promise you, they won't be able to stand the heat. That prime property sits right above Lake Union. They don't want their piece of the American Dream to include living next to Black folks, but they can't admit it."

After the garage doors were painted with the derogatory statement and the real issue exposed, it was discovered that several neighboring complexes had also created mother-in-law units, albeit rented to White residents. Once again, Daddy prevailed, and the DCLU granted him a variance to legalize the additional housing.

I was certain that, like some of the families I had encountered in my high school, there were bigots who believed their housing values diminished when Black families moved into their neighborhood. This continues today. According to a report in CNN Business (Alcorn, 2021), the average home in a primarily Black neighborhood is $46,000 less than a comparable home in a primarily White neighborhood. This research was conducted using value estimates for more than seven million homes that were listed and sold between 2013 and 2021 nationwide. Over the years, I have been asked over the phone how many Blacks reside at the property prior to scheduling an appointment. Apparently, my phone voice did not reveal my race, and the potential applicant did not know they were talking to a Black owner/operator.

THE PENDULUM SWINGS

In Seattle, the fight for rent control persists. In my view, rent control makes any existing housing shortage worse. It hurts the very population it was intended to help. When rent controls are in place, tenant competition for what little housing remains heats up. In addition, housing providers are not motivated to improve properties if their rent is not keeping up with inflation.

Recently, a law was on the docket to have a maximum late fee of $10 on delinquent tenants. It costs more to go to the movies than it does to pay the penalty for tardy rent payments, and a landlord now must wait longer before they can demand late payments.

Let's look at the laws from when my parents operated and today, in a side-by-side comparison, so you can see the pendulum swing.

Old Rules	New Rules
If a tenant did not pay rent, a landlord could give the resident a 3-day notice to pay or vacate. This would be followed by a court date and a motion to show cause, allowing the renter to explain why the rent was withheld. Then it was probable the judge would sign a writ of restitution, setting a date for the sheriff to do a physical eviction.	The tenant is given 14-day notice, allowing them 11 additional days to stay rent free and extending the time until the process goes to court. A nonpaying resident can potentially stay for a month for free.

Old Rules	New Rules
Once a lease was ended, housing providers had the right to increase rent to whatever the market rate would bear.	The landlord must give a minimum of 180 days' notice prior to a housing cost increase, even if it's $10. If it's 10% or more and your tenant meets income requirements, you may trigger the Economic Displacement Relocation Assistance (EDRA) if the tenant moves out.
Landlords had the right to determine their own pet policy and choose whether to allow pets or not.	Emotional-support animals are not considered pets and cannot be prohibited from units. Residents can move in with a doctor's letter. Many abuse this rule, obtaining fake letters. A housing provider cannot charge a deposit or additional rent for any damages caused by an emotional-support animal.
Housing providers had the right to choose whom they rented their property to.	Fair Chance Housing dictates housing providers cannot deny any renter based on criminal history.
Landlords could take multiple applications and determine which party was best suited for them to rent their properties to.	First in Time Ordinance requires landlords to offer rental agreements to the first qualified applicant to submit a complete application. Landlords must date and timestamp applications and screen in chronological order. Landlords must provide 48 hours for a response to an offer of a rental prior to proceeding to the screening of the next applicant.

Old Rules	New Rules
Landlords could determine if they wanted to rent to a subsidized housing occupant.	Landlords cannot deny housing because a renter's income comes from a source other than employment, such as a Section 8 Housing Certificate. The Housing Certificate mandates an annual inspection. Should the resident cause damage, the landlord is held liable, and the rent is withheld until repairs are complete.
A landlord could charge a deposit sufficient to cover damage. The costs of renovating an apartment on move-out, including flooring replacement, painting, lock changes, and any normal wear and tear and cleaning fees, generally always exceed a deposit.	The security deposit and fees combined cannot equal more than 1 month's rent.
The landlord determined who was allowed to occupy the rental.	Roommate Law allows renters to add immediate family, or one additional nonfamily roommate or immediate family of the additional roommate.

Housing providers must continue to challenge laws that eliminate their ability to operate and do their job efficiently. Being a landlord is my livelihood. Any business where a service is offered, compensation is mandated. If you dine at a restaurant, you pay for your meal. If you seek legal advice, you pay your attorney. If you get medical attention, the doctor's hours are billed. Imagine whatever profession you are in and at your expected pay date, you are told there is a moratorium on your fees. That is precisely what occurred for many housing providers during the pandemic, when a moratorium on evictions was put in place.

Shelter is a basic human need. But who is responsible for providing and paying for said accommodations?

GET UP AND GET ON IT

- KYS: know your shit. Laws are always changing. Stay up to date and get involved in your local real estate chapters, city council, and state policies and be your own advocate.

- Laws change frequently, and it's imperative to stay abreast of news both locally and nationally.

- Join your local agencies if you are in real estate; check out your local landlord periodicals and landlord associations.

- Hire a qualified attorney and perhaps keep him or her on speed dial.

- You must also stay up to date on developments in Fair Housing.

- Know which issues you're going to be prepared to take a stand on and decide how far you'll be willing to go to fight for your rights as a housing provider.

9

THE FAMILY
BUSINESS

I was born in Seattle, the beauty the scene
You came from Detroit when you were only eighteen
In search of a better life
You found a model partner and wife
I was born a privileged child raised in Catholic schools, private and elite,
I missed the education you got in the street
You've coached me to protest and make wrongdoings right
Lenders, laws, and lunatics, lessons learned in the fight
To make things happen, think out of the box and be innovative
How many properties have you bought where the financing was creative?
I tried to sell real estate, the conventional clown
You had another program, buy it with zero down
The ship has been sailing, we've got millions and mink
Our family business is the Titanic, but hey, didn't that sink?
Ain't no givin' in and no givin' out, it's been our lifelong motto
It's been our winning ticket and our family lotto
The neighborhood is changing, they call it gentrification
Housing costs on the rise, a part of urban inflation
I study and apply the necessary factors
Keeping negativity at bay and all the detractors
I say give me credit,
the response is, I'll never get it
You claim you've got so much more teaching to do
Lessons in refinance and the costs of renovations to review
What's it worth to fight with your own?
I'm not the enemy, I'm just grown
Class is over, pass the baton
I've got what it takes to carry on
You call me dummy, but of one thing I'm smart
We've got a difference of mind, but a sameness of heart
I Love You, Daddy

—Dana Frank

Family-owned businesses are the backbone of the American economy. According to familybusinesscenter.com, family businesses account for 64% of US gross domestic product, generate 62% of the country's employment, and account for 78% of all new job creation. I respect the history and hard-fought legacy that my parents created during turbulent racial, social, and economic times to create our family business while waiting on the world to change. In 2022, I created National Black Family in Business Day (National Day Archives, n.d.) to amplify and celebrate the contributions of Black family-owned businesses to our society. The economic impact by minority-owned family businesses is growing. Black-family-owned and -operated businesses should be celebrated and recognized for their contribution to society. I have watched many Black family-owned businesses over the years, and in Seattle, I have participated in Black Dollar Days where we come together and support these establishments. A National Day to highlight it in the press locally or nationally will continue to shed light on the hard work so many families do, which often goes unnoticed. My desire is to highlight the legacy and benefits of how working within your own family can change the trajectory of several generations.

That said, transition to the next generation in family business can be one of the greatest challenges in working with those you love. A multitude of issues need to be considered as the years go by and your family as well as your business grow. Issues such as ego, illness, new spouses, entitlement, equitable disbursements, greed, and expectations all at some point will likely need to be addressed. Many of my friends are established generational business owners, and they are now at the age where they're working on their succession plans.

Willingness to Participate

Often, parent-child relationships are combative, even without the complicating element of a working relationship. Do your children have the appetite, stamina, and desire to participate in the family business? Are you assuming, making a wish, or do you know the answer because you've asked them?

I was devastated when my son was graduating from the University of Washington with a degree from Foster School of Business. I had assumed that after graduation he would move out of his fraternity and come to work with the family. Christmas morning of his senior year, after we opened our gifts, Brett said he had an announcement. He shared that he had decided to move to Chicago, Illinois, and go to work for a friend's gaming company.

"You can't do that!" I shrieked, stumbling over our unwrapped gifts. I threw a tantrum and every obstacle I could summon to dissuade him. "It's freezing in Chicago. You are giving up all of what we've worked for all these years to go to Illinois and drive a Prius and sell slot machine games to local dive bars! You know what I have taught. You are either building for yourself or building for someone else."

The tears strolled down my face as I found myself standing at the Delta gate waving goodbye as Brett took off for his chi-town move. Perhaps my daughter, Taryn, 8 years Brett's junior, would assume stewardship of the business. It was too early to tell. I found myself repeating my father's words, "This is my sweat and your equity."

I often told Taryn that my menopause trumped her puberty. During her teen years, we argued about whether and how I was forcing her to engage, appreciate, and participate in our business. When she was in her high school years, she took a job working in public relations and marketing. That experience benefited our company, as what she learned there, she now applies for us. The experience of working for others also confirmed her entrepreneurial spirit. As she prepared for graduation, on her own volition, she decided to get her real estate license to get a better understanding of the real estate market.

I now tease my son that when he decided to move to Chicago, he became my error and not my heir. Brett spent 3 years in Chicago and eventually came home to assume leadership of the family business. When he left, I didn't know what the future held, but I had to grant him the decision to determine his own path.

Earning Our Keep

I was born into the real estate investment business, and I now know my upbringing was different than most. From the time we were in elementary school, Daddy felt we all needed to earn our keep and, more importantly, understand what we were building. My two sisters and I started with simple tasks such as riding in the car with extermination companies to allow entry to treat units from infestation. This exercise also allowed us to inspect the condition of the units and see how each resident had been taking care of their unit.

By the time we reached junior high school, we'd each received our own master key. The master key unlocks multiple doors, and we had all our properties keyed to the same Weiser lock system. We knew the importance of keeping that key guarded because it opened the doors to many lives. We spent our summer vacations cleaning and removing filth from vacant units. My two sisters and I could take a can of oven cleaner and make a stove sparkle as if it were brand new. We had unsoiled all the models over the years—Whirlpool, Roper, General Electric—and all the range colors too: harvest gold, lime green, chocolate brown, and white. Daddy bought used appliances from Reasonably Honest Dave's shop, a second-hand store selling rebuilt and recycled appliances: manual-defrost refrigerators and non-self-cleaning stoves. After a thorough cleanout, we would leave an open carton of baking soda in the freshly cleaned icebox, still trying to kill the odor from Reasonably Honest Dave's shop. Daddy never allowed us to dispose of the soiled tray pans, which could take hours of scrubbing. He felt it was a waste of money that elbow grease could cut. We learned to remove wallpaper by using a spray bottle of equal parts vinegar and water and saturating the wall. We stripped antique furniture pieces, which were converted into sinks using steel wool and not going against the grain, to create a smooth finish. We knew the difference between flat paint and semi-gloss, which was preferred because it could be washed when a resident moved rather than having to repaint an entire unit. When the units were completely detailed, our final step was to change the deadbolt lock.

Mama often worried and argued with Daddy about her babies' safety while cleaning up these unoccupied places. Our father hired day workers from the labor halls. He also tended to pick up any able-bodied man who was not inebriated from skid row to do a day's work cleaning apartments or hauling debris. One time Daddy left my eldest sister, Tracie, with a transient day laborer whom he had picked up from First Avenue and took them to a vacant apartment where they were to conduct basic detailing. (A vacant unit had to be cleaned to Daddy's satisfaction, or we would stay and work until it was.) Tracie was 14 at the time and past puberty. All went well until the pock-faced man crept up behind her and tried to fondle her. Tracie had a broom in hand,

and she whacked him fiercely up and down. He didn't bother her again. When Daddy came to pick them up, the apartment was spotless and ready for rent.

Life was safer as we graduated to working in the home office. Within the business, my father discussed all property matters with us. We were sponges, eager to learn and dutiful in our efforts. Daddy had beaten the odds, and we were constantly reminded by him that, "God bless the child that's got her own."

FAMILY IN COURT

Before I became general managing partner of our family business, I found myself sitting in a courtroom next to my mother facing the biggest foe of our lives: my father. It was one of the most painful, stressful, and shameful experiences of my life. Painful because I had to separate the love, respect, and concern I had for my father with that of my mother and our future. Stressful because everything that they had built was on the line, with escalating legal fees from their impending divorce proceedings, a costly receiver managing our properties who didn't take the same care with maintenance and upkeep as we did and as a result they were in deteriorating condition. And finally, it was shameful because this was not the narrative of our family. How could a Black family who amassed millions of dollars in real estate over decades face off in a court battle that rivaled the movie *War of the Roses*?

Can you imagine sitting opposite your father, mother, sister, or brother in a court of law? You are in a no-win battle as you fight for an estate you helped build and simultaneously to lose the love of a family member. My father likened my mother's filing for a divorce to his favorite movie, *The Bridge over the River Kwai,* where the prisoners got so busy building the bridge, they forgot they were building it for the enemy.

There was no turning back. Sitting at the plaintiff's table on the second floor of the King County Courthouse, my mother and I inched closer together and clenched our sweaty hands as we turned to see the most consequential adversary of our lives enter the courtroom. I sheepishly eyed his camel overcoat as he placed it on the chair adjacent to his attorney. He settled in his seat and yelled across at our table, "Just can't take that knife out of my back!" Our attorney warned us not to react. My father's attorney attempted, to no avail, to calm his client. Daddy was in a rage.

Our relationship was a combination of father-daughter, teacher-student, boss-employee, doctor-patient, friend-friend, friend-foe, and partner-partner. It got more complicated during challenging times when I did not agree with his ruthless tactics. I found his iron fist and alpha-male leadership style difficult. He was an admitted male chauvinist surrounded by women, and his constant grievance was that we allowed "bitchology," the study of complaining, to get in the way of his efforts to build our company. I am living proof and now accept that my father *did* have a method to his madness. But it was far from easy. I respect that he was a Fire Starter who had a vision and acted upon it and that it was no easy battle for him, either.

In 1974, long before the pendulum swung to favor tenants' rights over an owner's, the *Seattle Sun* newspaper featured my father on the front page with the caption, "Gerald Frank: Portrait of a Landlord." The piece described the story of an unemployed couple who had contacted the paper after they reportedly couldn't pay the rent and couldn't find another place to live. They didn't know who the owner or landlord was and were hoping the paper could help. The *Sun* did its homework, learning not only that Gerald Frank was owner of the property, but that his name was attached to a long list of civil actions, from property line disputes to building code violations, filed at the courthouse. The paper also reported that my father had a file full of complaints at the Seattle Tenants Union. Explaining why the Union had never, at that time, attempted to organize at any one of his properties, the story quoted a union staff person as saying, "He's too hot to handle." It's who he was.

But he was also more than that. Every year, our family took a cross-country drive, which my father insisted would be educational. We visited Mount Rushmore in South Dakota, toured Alcatraz in San Francisco, Pearl Harbor in Hawaii, and saw Old Faithful at Yellow National Park. On one trip while driving through Montana after we went from my father's hometown, Detroit, to Mama's birthplace, Chicago, we hit a deer. It was a forceful impact and left our Cadillac smashed. After we cleaned off the carcass at a gas station, Daddy drove us straight through the states to get us to the Robert Taylor Homes projects on the south side of Chicago. I can still smell the stench of the urine-filled elevators as my father held my arm as my siblings and I toured with our parents through the largest housing project in the United States. The Robert Taylor Homes were infested with pests and rats, and the drug abuse, gang violence, and poverty among the more than 27,000 inhabitants was an awakening for my 8-year-old self.

My father preached that we must always understand our privilege, and this was one of my earliest lessons on why we had to provide Black housing, to fight for equality, and to expose injustice. He always insisted on giving us a front row seat to how America lived versus giving us a sheltered upbringing.

The case over, I chose to reflect on the fact that my father was only operating with the tools that had been available to him and that he did his best. Eventually Daddy and I were able to resolve our issues, and we maintained a very close relationship until he died at the young age of 64 from heart disease and kidney failure. His gravestone reads: "A Man of Property and Prosperity. Jazz Man, Landlord, Father."

THE ROLES WE PLAY

As a wife, mother, daughter, sister, friend, entrepreneur, chef, counselor, teacher, financier, therapist, doctor, hair stylist, and caretaker, I embrace many roles in my life. Being the youngest in my family has afforded me the advantage of learning from my elder sisters and extended family members. I have witnessed both triumphs and hardships, including experiences with drug addiction, incarceration, loss, financial crises, and health issues. The measure of my success lies in how well-prepared I am to face challenging times and embrace the joys life offers.

The responsibilities and pressures of fulfilling these roles can sometimes feel overwhelming, necessitating compromise. For instance, my marriage does not adhere to the traditional model, as my husband and I live in separate states due to work and family commitments. Despite the distance, we make a concerted effort to see each other every two weeks. This requires patience, compromise, and hard work. However, our reunions are always joyful, and our relationship remains vibrant. As part of the sandwich generation, I am currently supporting my mother as she enters a stage of life where she requires more attention, while my children are launching their own lives and careers. It is an honor for me to give back to my mother and cherish the time we spend together, as she is not only my parent but also my best friend. Family always comes first, and I fiercely protect their well-being. Hence, I take on various roles and carry many titles. I firmly believe that my own happiness is intertwined with the well-being of my family, which includes every member, not just my children.

Assuming the role of the chief financial officer for my family is a significant commitment, accompanied by its own pressures. I am determined to instill the mindset of getting up and getting things done to secure a prosperous legacy. Each morning, my team, which now consists of my adult children and our maintenance foreman, all gather together to check in and plan our schedules for the day. We support and rely on each other, sharing the same goals and working together as a cohesive partnership. Our individual passions, goals, and desires align as we strive to cross the finish line together.

So, what happens when families in business have disagreements that result in estrangement, lawsuits, and ensuing battles? The results can destroy your life and livelihood. When my parents divorced after 30 years of marriage, the stakes were high. My sisters and I were limited partners, and had my parents not settled, the entire estate could have been jeopardized and lost.

Unfortunately, while business values and family values overlap, they do not necessarily align. At least not seamlessly. For most of us, our daily work persona is very different from the role that we play in family life. But in a family business, role separation is built with blurred lines. If Dad is the boss, when he talks to one of his employees, he may also be addressing one of his children. The expectations we have of members of our family—that we put the family's interest first, that we take care of each other— may conflict with the goal of maximizing economic return. To that extent, social roles are not always aligned. Family business has a built-in conflict.

My father, as the founder of the company, was the self-appointed ruler. He was the best teacher and fiercest foe for anyone who threatened his program. His method worked for many years, until technology, modern principles, and our maturing family all rendered his street-sense operation obsolete. I understand that his roots and battles shaped him, leading him to make often unethical decisions; however, I could not and do not operate or run a business the way he did. My father started without a cell phone and running the books manually. As times changed and more tools became accessible, he had a hard time relinquishing control of his old-school practices. As our family matured, we all had our own methods and ideas on what would make the business sustainable and grow. My sisters, fed up with my father's often unethical practices, decided to leave the business. I vowed to partner with my mother, and we shared a clear vision on how our future would evolve.

My mother and I have worked seamlessly for nearly 40 years because we have always shared the same outlook and long-term plan. And that plan is to build and preserve legacy. We also have successfully carved out roles for each of us that reflect personal preferences and fulfill operational needs. For example, I personally enjoy renting the units. My son is great at community outreach and testifying against bills that affect our operation. My mother has a keen eye for design and bill paying.

SUCCESSION PLANNING

Conflict can arrive from any direction, but succession often poses a serious challenge for family business. If a family business is to survive, each generation must eventually cede control to the next. And yet many family businesses fail to plan for succession, dealing only with the issue during the death of or incapacitation of a controlling family member. Also, parents may hesitate when faced with the choice whether to treat all children equally or transfer control to the most able member of the next generation.

We had an estate attorney who clearly defined our family partnership agreement, and thus my sisters and I were awarded our shares of the estate.

I learned that regardless of my own desires, you must allow your heirs to follow their own paths. If you are going into the real estate investment business with your family, you need to consider numerous conditions.

GET UP AND GET ON IT!

- Engage your children early and often in discussions about the family business. Learning about business and establishing a work ethic can and should start early.

- Listen to your offspring and accept whether they are interested in carrying the torch from what you began.

- Understand personality conflicts early and determine if a family partnership is feasible. Have a partnership agreement in place. Just because it is family doesn't mean you won't have fallouts and legal concerns.

- Determine duties and allow each family member to take charge of an area of their own expertise.

- Hire a lawyer, consultant, or other third party to help you lay out a succession plan.

- Articulate long-term goals and ensure everyone is on the same page.

- Discuss prenuptial agreements and foster a familial understanding because when your children marry it introduces legal complications.

- There can be only one captain to a ship, so who will navigate? This person has the overall decision-making obligation for when to buy, refinance, sale, rent to a prospective tenant, and more.

- Hold each other accountable.

10

FEEL THE FEAR AND DO IT ANYWAY

When we started this journey much was unknown

Daddy no longer at the helm sitting on the family throne

'This business is a man's world', we were told, 'Don't do it, you'll be eaten alive'

Contractors, problem tenants, financing, and making mortgage payments to survive

We had a decision to sink or swim

They doubted us, but we made it without him

Daddy had a street tough way, but Mama had a diplomatic other

I have never doubted my decision to partner with my mother

From behind his glasses, he taught us all he knew

We magnified and multiplied—our family and business grew

We made it and didn't even realize upon the arrival of our destination

Perseverance and hard work pays not procrastination

Seventy years and counting, this legacy created

Gentrified and refurbished properties which were once obliterated

Mama changed the narrative of her birth story, mine, and of off-spring yet to be

Because behind her glasses, the vision has always been 20/20 perfection that she sees

It's from behind Mama's glasses that this story will continue to be told

And repeat itself for future generations to augment and behold

—Dana Frank

Many of the stories I have shared have revolved around my father and his vision to get up and get on it. But I must share the backbone of our family and the reason we have soldiered on for seven decades, and it is the warrior woman I was blessed to call my mother.

My mother, age 91 as of this writing, is still defying the clock and is an active participant in the company. She and I continue to

Theresa Frank on her 90th birthday

maintain the thriving rental business with all the properties she along with my father started collecting in 1950. We continued to purchase, refinance, and expand, in conjunction with my son, Brett, today. As our mission has always been, we provide quality, affordable housing.

My mother and I became business partners in June 1989. I was 25 and my mother was 56 years old the day the judge signed my parents' divorce decree. When we walked out of that courtroom, we had substantial debt and legal fees. My mother's original attorney had been bribed by my father and tried to convince my mother to take an inequitable settlement. We later discovered this miscarriage of justice and had to find a reputable attorney, which we found in our friend, Mark Olson.

My father's reputation in our city was that he was a notorious, often ruthless businessman one did not want to cross. We feared that without my father's protection, our safety was at risk, and we would not survive. Once my mother and I attended a Seattle Super Sonic basketball game at our city's arena. After I put cash in the parking meter, a man appeared and stepped between us and the machine, took a hanger with gum on the end, and siphoned out the cash we had just put in. It was evening and getting dark. There were a few people scurrying nearby to get to the game, however, no one was paying attention. I stood in horror as this man brazenly stole our cash right in front of our eyes. My mother seemed unafraid, and in a strong, unyielding voice, demanded the thief give us back our money. At that point, the thief turned to face us, slowly and menacingly, and said, "The only reason I am going to respect and not harm you is because you are Gerald Frank's wife." Neither my mother nor I had ever seen this man before. Every day it was as if we were living in a fishbowl, and we had to constantly be aware of our surroundings and our security.

I have now passed the age my mother was when we started out and I have experienced much of her life as a divorced mother and working woman. I often wonder where she inherited the strong determination, grit, and fight, still at age 91 today, to get up and get on it. I would be remiss not to share that her faith, her good genes, and her daily vitamins may play their part; however, I believe her greatest attribute is her optimism. I am fortunate to benefit from her strength and eternal outlook for good.

Even in our most dire moments when money was scarce, we never sought handouts from family or friends, except on one occasion—and that was short term, less than 30 days, and it was secured with a piece of property and interest was paid as we awaited financing. We had to figure out how to forge a path as if other resources were not available. We would joke with each other as some weeks we would take home enough money for Mama to have a Lean Cuisine, and we would laugh when I said, "That's a splurge! Swanson's frozen dinners are cheaper."

During those years of struggling financially, under Mama's hopeful outlook we never lost sight of what we were building. Once our custom 1976 Cadillac convertible caught fire. The car had hundreds of thousands of miles on the odometer. The doors and ill-fitting roof rattled noisily as we drove around our properties. We arrived at one of our rental homes and parked as the car overheated and soon a blaze erupted from under the hood. We stood by, smiling, and looking at the bright side: and that was the fact that the car was insured, and we would receive a payout. Suddenly, to our dismay, a neighbor who had been working in her garden ran over with a hose and called the fire department. The damn car was salvaged. We eventually junked the vehicle and financed a Jeep Cherokee, which provided more reliable transportation.

Another time during our financial distress we hired a contractor. His craftsmanship was superb, and his fees were affordable. We left him in charge of a project while we took a much-needed trip to Germany to visit my sister who had given birth to a son with serious medical issues. Upon our return to the States, we discovered the contractor had spent the money earmarked for our project and the work had not commenced. Turns out our crafty contractor was a drug addict who couldn't resist the temptation our leaving him in charge offered. Lesson learned: you must stay present to win. We were finally able to pull together the money we needed to restore the gutted house, which upon completion became the *Post-Intelligencer*'s Personality Home of the Week. This was a weekly feature in our local newspaper showcasing homes for sale. We were eager to cash out, even enlisting the help of Saint Joseph. In our Catholic faith, Saint Joseph is the patron saint of workers, happy marriages, and real estate. We followed the steps: obtaining a small statue of him, burying him in the yard a few feet from the for-sale sign, with his head pointing down and facing toward the house. We said our little novena and hoped for the best.

The house didn't sell, and we ended up renting it. The statue remained in the ground and the property sold 25 years later at a hefty price. Had Saint Joseph answered our request when we planted him, we would not have garnered the huge windfall when the market skyrocketed. Thanks, Saint Joseph.

Theresa Frank has gone by many titles and worn many hats from the day she was born into a family on welfare. She's been a caretaker, nurse's aide, telephone operator, elevator attendant, department store window dresser, bartender, nightclub owner, real estate magnate, model, wife, sister, mother, and grandmother. When my kids were growing up, we affectionately nicknamed her "Precious" as she's been the treasure that keeps our family grounded.

Co-parenting my children with my mother as we built our business was a journey filled with shared experiences. She was there beside me, attending swim lessons, joining me for Ms. Jeanne's Reading Before School, and accompanying me to Kumon math classes. We spent countless hours in the rain cheering at soccer games and swim and track competitions and enduring long ballet classes and recitals, all while managing our business and showing apartments. The investment of time and effort has yielded tangible results.

My children experienced firsthand the saying, "It takes a village," as they were profoundly impacted by their grandmother. I'm moved by the love, respect, and admiration my children display for her, their bond with her is a source of immense joy in my life. My mother has faced fear straight on, and she has always been the last one standing. While building our family business, she was the key to keeping us out of bankruptcy and cleaning up after trouble created by my father or by a system designed to hold her back.

I often marvel at her resilience and strength when I think of how she had to testify before the grand jury. Our family had been accused of overcharging low-income Housing and Urban Development tenants their subsidized rent when we rented the units furnished. Mama took the witness stand and persevered.

When my father forged the bank president's signature on an insurance claim check on a property that had burned down and reasoned it was his property to rebuild, the bank sued. And my mother was the one who negotiated the settlement.

When my mother divorced my father after 32 years of marriage, she was forced to face the fear of the unknown. Our business was on the brink of bankruptcy after the court-ordered receivership left the estate in ruin. We faced deadbeat and dangerous tenants.

We had guns pulled on us. We fought for loans to keep us afloat, even though they were often less than 50% LTV and at less than desirable interest rates.

As the matriarch of our family, she has weathered countless storms, including the loss of loved ones, health concerns, divorce and family lawsuits, estrangements, dealing with family members battling addiction and alcoholism, and enduring financial hardships. She pioneered a business career at a time when women were expected to be housewives and to focus solely on raising children. Through it all, she has exhibited remarkable resilience. Mama is not one to host pity parties; instead, she approaches each situation with a practical mindset. She carefully examines the circumstances, finds solutions, puts them to the test of her soul and scientific reasoning, and commits herself to getting things done. Her unwavering faith and optimistic outlook have not only served her well but also influenced our entire family.

Mama has been my example that when you remove the "e" from fear, you'll go far. Today, as we walk through buildings that could have easily been lost in the battles, I know it is because of her perseverance that we still stand. And we stand tall.

Because I was raised by such a strong role model, I have learned from her example. I have been that vulnerable, uncertain, and fearful woman who only had her self-belief, work ethic, and faith to pull her through. As an adult, I've never been one who puts my future in the hands of someone else. I bank on me. And if I lose, I use it as a lesson on how to get it right the next time.

When I sat in that courtroom facing my father with everything on the line, I knew the outcome could have gone either way. I was 25 and seriously considering my options. I had applied for a job as a flight attendant with Alaska Airlines. I figured I was personable, I had good people skills, and I loved to travel, so the job would be a good fit. But in my gut, I knew real estate was embedded in every fiber of my being.

After my parents' divorce and we flirted with bankruptcy and our family fell apart, I didn't have financial resources, but I had drive. And I had desire. I was dating a local football star, and like many impressionable young women, I could have easily been allured by the luxury lifestyle those hefty contracts command. I had sold him a waterfront penthouse, a three-bedroom, three-bathroom home equipped with an elevator that opened privately to his unit. We had traveled to San Francisco to buy furniture and art custom fit for the space. The garage held his Jaguar and a limited-edition SUV. Our vacations included him being inducted into the Pro Bowl in Hawaii and Las Vegas for awards shows. He was a kind, Christian man who thanked God for every touchdown. That could have been my future.

I broke up with him during my parents' pending divorce. I had no idea what the future held, but I followed my gut. Everyone thought I made a poor decision when I walked out of the relationship and on him, and people suggested I was bat shit crazy. Like my parents before me had been, I was Black and broke, but not broken. I put the pedal to the metal and became my own kind of Fire Starter.

Was I afraid when my financial security was stripped from under me? Absolutely. Did I have FOMO—extreme fear of missing out—when my football player married, and I knew I had to make it on my own? You bet! Did I miss the comforts of the multi-million-dollar lifestyle? Without a doubt. But guess what? I knew I had the tools to create it on my own.

Some of my most enduring and endearing memories are those days when my mom and I were hitting it early and hard and realizing that failure was not an option. There were hard-scrabble days when we invested all available money back into the properties. After mortgages and expenses were paid, we may have dined on canned soup, but we had a plan. Through the banking hardships and begging to get financing, we studied, and we found our way. I read about banks giving moratoriums, and my mother and I decided to take a local banker out to lunch. When we shared our plight, that a divorce and receivership had left our properties in extreme disrepair and we needed to renovate to improve the resident quality and income, he gave in and agreed to help. That act alone bought us time as we went 1 year without making a mortgage payment on our larger complexes and the interest was tacked to the end of the note.

We've had tenants tear up our properties, some purposely vandalized and others just by lack of concern. We've seen family fallouts and struggles to make the monthly mortgage and expenses, the pandemic, insane laws that favor tenants over housing providers, and unjust lawsuits. Through it all, one thing I know for certain: real estate investing is a powerful way to create real wealth. It may take some years, but those are going to fly by anyway, so it's like putting cash in the bank, but with a better interest rate.

We have dealt with every facet in the changing face of the apartment rental business. Deadbeat and problem tenants are an unavoidable part of our operation. Safety first and as a woman in business, I know too many stories of those who prey on single females showing units. As a rule, we do not show an apartment alone. We have faced guns being pulled on us, feeling fortunate to have escaped with our lives. We have been threatened by gang members who have moved in with their senile grandmothers and started selling drugs. We have been sued by opportunistic tenants who fake a claim. There have been break-ins, thefts, homeless camping out in the laundry room seeking shelter from the cold, property fires, and violent domestic abuse cases. In our most trying circumstances, I have had to call our police department to intervene.

And still the rewards make it all worth it. The sacrifices my parents made ignited not only a lifestyle and future for their heirs, but also a passion and platform for me to share with others that changing their circumstances is possible. As my children and I walk the properties that my Fire Starter parents, by hook and crook, started investing in over seven decades ago, I can't help but think of the quote: "Plant a tree today, so that even though you may not enjoy the shade, your children and their grandchildren will."

Each of our properties has a story, and I've already spoken here about the saying, "Don't fall in love with your properties," but I have. Our family home, which the seller was holding out for a Black buyer in 1963 during the segregation era, is in an area now gentrified and worth tens of millions more. There was the HUD building that became a condominium, housing young urban professionals and no longer the Section 8 residents from our early ownership days. I have fond memories of a house my father bought for $30,000 cash after I refused to present the seller with an offer, who to all our surprise made the deal because he needed the cash and didn't want to wait for conventional financing. There's the 35-unit building I purchased 22 years ago in an area that was in transition. Fast forward two decades, the neighborhood has become the most vibrant of all our properties with the light rail, PCC Grocery, and sought-after new construction.

Real estate was our vehicle, and it has consistently remained a steady and successful investment throughout time. The fact that real estate is a tangible, physical asset and, unlike most jobs where your paycheck is mandated by your health among other factors, investing in real property provides a constant value. Although the journey to seeing a return on your investment may take some years, it is a safe bet as, regardless of the economy, homes will always be needed.

As a family who has been in the rental housing business for more than 70 years and as a woman who has worked as the general managing partner for the past 25 years, I have weathered recessions, a pandemic, high interest rates, and ever-changing laws that highly favor the tenant over the housing provider. However, despite the hardships, real estate has never failed me. The demand for rental units increases as property values continue to rise. The favorable tax benefits, write-offs, and owning an appreciating asset make real estate investing appealing.

I took up skiing as an adult. The fun, adrenaline, beautiful scenery, and workout all enticed me. The fear was intense, at least at the start because, as the saying goes, it's hard to teach an old dog new tricks. Lesson after lesson, my confidence grew as I morphed from wedging to parallel turns. The adrenaline reached all-time highs on days when I glided with ease down more challenging slopes without fail or falling. I felt accomplished after a long day on the lifts, with my legs aching from a much-needed workout.

One day while vacationing with friends in Sun Valley and enjoying the après ski and a warm cocktail in the lodge, my husband smiled at me and said, "Skiing is the most fun one can have with their clothes on." I disagree. Walking through one of my renovated projects and handing over the keys to a responsible resident who is paying me handsomely for my efforts is by far the most fun I can have with—or without—my clothes on!

Reflecting on the times we struggled is a reminder that although things don't happen always on demand, or when we feel the most urgent need, they do happen when the time is right. It is always heartwarming to reflect on how far we have come and now we can really laugh and smile back at our naïve, bold, hopeful, and optimistic selves. Every part of our history is a treasure. Two Black women, a mother and daughter who partnered on faith and belief in themselves, through family turmoil, lawsuits, financial constraints, and health concerns, we have survived and thrived. We banked on ourselves. Mama and I have lived together for most of our lives. She's the first one I speak to in the morning and the last one at night and I wouldn't want it any other way. The way I see it, I know her literally and figuratively from the inside out and there is no one I trust more. If you are fortunate to have a healthy family relationship and work with your own, as you prosper, you will enjoy the fruits of generational legacy and change the narrative for generations to come.

Real estate was my first real love. It has taken care of me. I love what I do. I love being my own boss. I know my business from the crown to the ground, and thus, I enjoy the perks of setting my own schedule. I am proud of my family and our accomplishment: providing quality and affordable housing.

My father has been gone more than 25 years. I don't know what his intention was or if he even understood the impact that his decision to invest at age 18 in his first property would have on our family lineage when he got started. "It's my sweat and your equity," I can still hear him say. I take those words to heart more than ever now as I prepare to pass the baton to the next generation. My hope is that my children, as stewards of the fruits of their grandparents' labor, will keep the legacy going. My gift is not only for my children, but for all those young minds out there wondering how to create annuity income and generational wealth: through understanding the power of investing.

If I had to talk to my 25-year-old self, I would say over and again: the struggle is temporary, enjoy the ride, and believe the best is yet to be. Each day is a gift, so be present. Be patient. Don't suffer fools. Study. Network. Be open. Live healthily. Spend quality time with those you love. Set boundaries. Don't accept *no*. Continue to grow and learn every day. Be charitable. Smile. Laugh. Travel. Invest. Be your own Master Key. Change the narrative. Get up and get on it.

I pray that you will start today. Connect with money partners, network, ask your family, friends, find people at church or the gym, open the dialogue, and discuss investing. Study your neighborhoods. Spend your weekends attending open houses. Get your real estate license or befriend a realtor to see firsthand what is happening in the market and pay attention to trends. Join your local chapter of rental housing professional networks. Take classes on renovating. Collect home improvement magazines. Study the rental market and learn what the median rents bear.

Cash erodes. Equity grows. Invest and may every venture be an adventure for you and yours. Get up and get on it!

We must preserve what has value and disregard what does not. If you are not satisfied with your current situation, remember that investing is an opportunity that can change your future and that of those you love. I'm at the point in my life when I am reflecting on my legacy. When I coach tennis to homeless little Black girls or host my annual holiday drive fundraiser that supports primarily minority children in the foster care system, I want my legacy to be that they see me in their eyes: I want them to see someone who looks like them and has navigated the system to live like the 1%.

GET UP AND GET ON IT

- Don't look back; you aren't going that way.

- Expect setbacks and keep going anyway. There will undoubtedly be hardships, loan denials, partner disputes, financial hardships, and barriers to break down. Every business, I don't care how financially well off it may be, has experienced setbacks.

- Choose to view obstacles as opportunities.

- Sleep when you're dead. There will be days when you are exhausted, of course. Allow time to recharge your mind and body but utilize your downtime to help further your goals.

- Make time to work out, whether it's a walk, an hour at your local gym, or join a tennis group.

11

ACHIEVING IT ALL

Where does she find the energy?
Seamlessly weaving what's all on her plate with synergy
Business, friends, family, travel, a workout and giving
Slow down, they say, but she's too busy living
She knows time is fleeting
But says yes to another meeting
Because one platform begets another
It's wisdom instilled from her father and mother
Time is money, so don't waste it please
Another deal done, expedited with ease
Not a day ends that she doesn't look back and smile
Because she makes sure every day is worthwhile
She has a reason to live, love, and laugh
Daily she stays the course on her vision and path
She's every woman taking care of life and biz
Independent and empowered, that is what it is
Confident, accomplished, and always standing tall
Don't give her a portion, she's having it all.

—Dana Frank

Many people often observe my life and remark, "You need to slow down," or "How do you manage it all?" Or they tease me and say I'm spread too thin, like butter, but truth be told, I wouldn't have it any other way.

The truth is, staying busy comes naturally to me. I attribute this to my upbringing and my father's belief in the now-debunked myth that humans use only 10% of their brains. He instilled in me the importance of taking action every day. Dale Carnegie's best-selling 1936 book, *How to Win Friends and Influence People,* referred to this 10% brain usage, also reinforcing the notion that an idle mind is the devil's workshop. Consequently, I was raised to stay engaged. My father would often say, "If you do nothing, nothing is going to happen."

Because we now know, thanks to research reported in an article by Daniel Murrell, MD, published in medicalnewstoday.com on February 27, 2018, that in fact most of our brains are utilized most of the time. Thus, with practical and common-sense practices such as maintaining a healthy diet, regular exercise, mental stimulation, and adequate sleep, I believe that having it all is a matter of choice.

PURPOSE AND RESILIENCE

Having it all requires sacrifice and a proactive approach to life. It entails implementing preventive measures and preparing for the inevitable obstacles that will arise. Like having an evacuation plan for emergencies like fire or earthquake, we also need to have contingency plans in place for our health and financial well-being. This often involves prioritizing the needs of others over our own and organizing tasks based on their importance. This pursuit sometimes includes sleepless nights and working while others are at play, all to attain a level of success that others may not reach. It encompasses practicing tough love while raising children and setting boundaries with both friends and foes. Moreover, it necessitates dedicating time for self-care and nurturing our own health, mind, and body. However, the most vital component of having it all is the determination to rise above the inevitable obstacles and accomplish tasks, no matter what comes our way.

Every day, I wake up with purpose, establish a list of goals, and strive to excel in each endeavor, regardless of its size. I prioritize my tasks based on urgency and importance, and I firmly believe in tackling the less desirable items earlier in the day. As a housing provider, I must be readily available to address my residents' concerns, just as I prioritize complaints, repairs, and worries based on their level of urgency.

To ensure accountability, I have implemented a monthly thirty-day review and assessment of my life. Since my birthday falls on August 26th, I consider the 26th of each month my personal new year. Instead of waiting an entire year to reflect and set new goals, I celebrate my accomplishments on the 26th of every month. This allows me to evaluate what I've achieved, and to identify areas where I can improve. You've likely heard that annual New Year's resolutions have a high failure rate. My monthly accountability practice helps me ensure my resolutions don't suffer a similar fate. And sometimes, my bright ideas turn into something.

TUTU TIME

In 2006, my mother and I introduced an innovative clip-on timepiece called Tutu Time, with the tagline, "Time That Goes Anywear!" Named after my mother's nickname, this patent-pending watch could discreetly clip onto an evening bag or be worn as a necklace. The Tutu Time watches gained significant media attention, with features in renowned publications such as InStyle, Ebony, Hollywood Life, and Nashville Lifestyles, as well as in local magazines. We even had the opportunity to appear on *The Big Idea with Donny Deutsch* show, although our big idea was overshadowed by a light-in-the-dark pooper scooper. Undeterred by this humbling television debut, I was determined to prove the merit of our timepieces and continued marketing them at every opportunity.

That's what I was doing nearly a year later at a charity event hosted by my uncle Quincy Jones in Beverly Hills when I first encountered JG Wentworth cofounder Gary Veloric and his wife, Nancy. Veloric is a serial entrepreneur and undoubtedly one of the most creative dealmakers of our time. That year, 2007, driven by his analytical prowess for complex transactions, his love for music, and incorporating business and creativity, Veloric founded the Red Stripe Plane Group.

Wearing a black mother-of-pearl stainless Tutu Time encrusted with diamonds, I shared with Gary the creation story of our unique watches. It was through this encounter that I learned the valuable lesson of embracing every venture as an adventure.

At Gary's invitation, my mother and I flew to Philadelphia, where he arranged a meeting for us at QVC, a home-shopping television channel owned by Qurate Retail Group. They presented us with a potential partnership opportunity. However, accepting their terms would have required compromising the quality of our time-pieces to meet their price criteria. They requested a drastic reduction in the retail price, which would have entailed purchasing a substantial amount of low-quality inventory and dealing with potential returns under their policy. Given the associated risks, my mom and I decided not to proceed. This decision was aligned with Gary's mindset of recognizing when a risk outweighs the potential reward.

Gary also envisioned a much brighter future for me than as a peddler of watches. In 2007, Gary's introductions lead me to add another role to my list and I joined the Newark Bears Baseball Team as the chief marketing officer. During my time with the team, we collaborated with Senator Cory Booker, who was then mayor of Newark, New Jersey, to revitalize the high-crime areas of downtown Newark and revive the last team affiliated with the historic Negro Leagues. Our efforts included bringing in notable figures like Colin Powell for the first pitch, Patti LaBelle to sing the National Anthem, and hosting hometown favorites such as Queen Latifah for an All-Star Game. We organized Legends' Nights, honoring baseball greats from Whitey Ford to Jackie Robinson. My time with the Newark Bears provided me with a remarkable experience, granting me a front-row seat to the world of entertainment, including the Grammy Awards, behind-the-scenes experiences in Nashville's recording studios, and meetings in Trump Tower with influential figures from the boxing and apparel industries.

Gary's journey showcases the power of determination, unconventional thinking, and the willingness to learn from both successes and failures.

WHAT I LEARNED FROM GARY ABOUT ACHIEVING IT ALL

Gary has been an incredible mentor and friend to me, teaching me invaluable lessons that continue to shape my life. Gary began his career working with his entrepreneurial father at Geriatric & Medical Companies, a publicly traded long-term-care company. However, Gary chose to forge his own path, stepping away from the shadow of his demanding father. Despite having a platform in the family business, Gary made the courageous decision to depart from it in 1992, without any substantial gain. In essence, he left it all to achieve it all.

Like Gary's pivotal decision to leave his father's business, I too took a leap of faith by walking away from what my father had built, ultimately finding myself in a courtroom opposite him. Although it was a challenging and risky move, it turned out to be a catalyst for my success, amplifying my life and creating generational wealth that would have likely been dissipated amid my parents' divorce.

Just like Gary, I have a penchant for deals and investments, often finding myself inundated with enticing opportunities. I've launched new ventures, including Tutu Time, the clip-on timepiece company, and I've invested in Tully's Coffee, Isabella Fiore Handbags, and even in fracking trucks in South Dakota. However, as Gary taught me, I never linger in the disappointment of deals that don't materialize into the next big thing. Instead, I embrace his philosophy and swiftly move on, continuously seeking new opportunities for growth.

Gary himself faced a significant financial setback with the Newark Bears and the Red Stripe Team. Nevertheless, he demonstrated his astuteness by recognizing the point at which investing more money in a failing venture would yield no further returns. In a similar vein, I transformed what could have been a failure with Tutu Time into a remarkable opportunity by connecting with Gary, leveraging his expertise, and turning it into a thriving platform.

Despite his accomplishments and philanthropic endeavors, Gary prefers to fly under the radar. Red Stripe Planes Group serves as a metaphor for his approach—a private airline for the US government that takes scientists to remote areas of the desert for top-secret research, with the only mark being a red stripe. Gary's impact has touched countless lives, often without people even realizing it. His endeavors include JG Wentworth, the name of a company he created to sound similar to JP Morgan, where the J and the G stood for Jew and Gentile reflecting the diverse religions of the two founders.

One of the most valuable lessons I've learned from Gary is his remarkable ability to listen attentively and thoroughly investigate every opportunity. Even to this day, I rely on his wisdom and bounce various ideas and opportunities off him. Whether it's venture capital deals like alcohol-infused popsicles, professional baseball kits, video instructions by major league players for pre-teens, or even seeking advice on finding a better refinance lender for my personal real estate, Gary assesses the potential upside and quickly identifies any red flags. His invaluable input is what makes him an exceptional mentor.

In essence, Gary's mentorship has been a source of inspiration and guidance, shaping my decision-making processes and propelling me toward success. I hold him in high regard not only as a mentor but also as a big brother and friend.

Success Is a Mindset

The email subject line read "Jackson Hole, Wyoming Jan 17-21, 2018." It was an invitation for me and my husband, Eric, to join Donald Thompson, CEO and founder of Maxwell Group and of Senior Living Communities, which owns and operates over 3400 units in six states with more than 2800 employees, at an executive leadership team event.

The location was the luxurious Four Seasons, a AAA five-star resort, and the itinerary included two days of skiing, a snowmobiling trip into Yellowstone, and a tasting of 100-point wines. Everything from ski instructors to help us with putting on our heated boots, to lift tickets, and well-appointed luxury rooms were all included in this amazing experience. Thompson ended the email with the inspiring words reflecting his philosophy of life, "Live long, live well, live!"

I've known Thompson through my husband's work as CEO of a public company that specializes in financing for senior housing. We've become great friends with Donald and his wife, Brenda, and we have enjoyed many trips and dinners together.

Thompson is one of the most charming, friendly, and likable people I've ever met. He is generous and always shows his gratitude to staff and service members. A true risk-taker, Donald has achieved amazing success in business, marriage, family, and friendships.

Thompson's philosophy in life and business shows his positive attitude, and it's that attitude, that mindset, that I believe is directly responsible for his success. Let me explain.

Donald grew up in a middle-class family in rural North Carolina. His father was a teacher who started building houses. His father had paid for his own college education, so he expected Donald to do the same. Donald worked hard at jobs that no one wanted over the summers. He cleaned houses, and laid insulation and poured foundations. He missed a lot of the social part of his young life, but he wanted to finish school and get his degree as fast as possible to stop the hard manual labor. He did it in two years instead of four. He navigated his tight financial budget while dating, telling his dates that he was on a diet so they would dine at all-you-can-eat salad bars. Of course, while dieting, alcohol was not to be consumed, so that helped keep his bill manageable.

With the skillset from his summer-college-fund construction work intact, Donald started his own home building business with a bank loan and some credit lines and turned it into a successful venture. Donald started in the care industry in 1980, when he built his first assisted living community.

But then the Reagan-era recession hit, and Donald lost everything. At the time, it was the most severe economic recession and was widely considered the most significant financial setback of our generation since World War II. He had to move with his wife and three young sons into his parents-in-law's house. Donald said eating peanut butter from a jar and living with his in-laws drove him to focus on how to fix things and get back on track.

Even when he told me about this difficult time in his life, I saw his positive attitude—his mindset of success—shine through. He said we all face bad situations in life, but he chooses to focus on the good. Donald told me about the worker who had to clean the horse stalls. Every day, the worker had to smell the horse manure, but he kept a happy attitude as he shoveled away because he thought there must be a horse somewhere. Like the worker, Donald found his horse and after bankruptcy, he got back on his horse and became one of the big players in the senior housing industry. He taught this grit and hard work ethic to his sons, who are now running his companies. He thinks his sons are motivated because they too remember the hard times when the family was broke.

Donald was not defeated by the economic disaster of that recession nor of the Pandemic. Over the past five decades, he has owned several companies which support our growing aging population with independent living, assisted living, dementia care, skilled nursing, rehab services, medical equipment and supplies, pharmacy and home health services.

My biggest takeaway from my meeting with Donald was that being successful is a mindset. He referenced the old saying, "If you believe you can or you believe you can't, either way you are probably right."

As we talked, I learned that Donald's lessons were not about how to make a lot of money, but how to remember the struggle and the fact that the good you do in the world comes back to you many times over. Which is really all about mindset.

MENTAL HEALTH CHECK

According to the Columbia University Department of Psychiatry, research suggests the adult Black community is 20% more likely than the White community to experience serious mental health problems (Vance, 2019), yet only one in three African Americans who need help actually receive it.

This is a disturbing statistic. Black people are often taught to not share their "dirty laundry." We're often told that other people either don't want to hear our problems or that the haters are glad to know we have them. I have watched friends binge eat to the point of obesity and drink alcohol in excess to mitigate their pain rather than seek medical or mental health attention. If someone you love was diagnosed with cancer, you wouldn't judge them for getting chemotherapy. The same sentiments should apply to getting therapy and mental wellness. I believe we in the Black community must come together to break the shame around mental health.

As a housing provider, I have witnessed time and again marginalized residents of color whose lives have unraveled. With the fentanyl, drug, alcohol, and homeless crises in Seattle, I have tried to help some residents get into treatment. The sad reality is not enough beds or medical staff are available, and the cost is prohibitive. A 5-day stay at a detox center ranges from $5,000 to $7,500. A month-long stay for recovery can cost from $20,000 to $50,000. Paying fees like this privately is often out of reach, and trying to navigate insurance is a challenge. We must address making treatment affordable and accessible as it will save lives. Unfortunately, I have had several residents commit suicide in circumstances like these, when they became so desperate and unable to find help.

The power of music to engage and stimulate the brain has been extensively studied by neuroscientists in recent decades using advanced techniques like fMRI and PET scanners. That's at least partially true when listening to music. But playing a musical instrument really activates areas of the brain, including the visual, auditory, and motor cortices. In her 2017 Ted Talk, "How Playing an Instrument Benefits Your Brain," Anita Collins describes the musician's activity as "like a full-body brain workout."

The connection between music and memory has also been consistently demonstrated in studies. I had a firsthand experience of this when I visited a close friend who suffered a stroke while performing on stage with Bruce Springsteen. The stroke left him with communication difficulties and impaired motor skills. However, during his rehabilitation, I noticed the calming effect that familiar jazz tunes had on him. Listening to this music brought the producer, composer, arranger, and musician a sense of comfort and familiarity.

Musicians have been an integral part of my life. I am married to a talented jazz guitarist who, despite music being his hobby, dedicates himself with passion to daily practice. Quincy Jones, my uncle and a legendary figure in the music industry, shares in his book, *12 Notes: On Life and Creativity*, that music is built on just 12 notes, emphasizing that it's how those notes are played that truly matters. He also believes that life revolves around rhythm, urging us to keep the music playing. Moreover, my father, who was recognized as one of Seattle's best organists and drummers in Paul de Barros' book, *Jackson Street After Hours*, instilled in me a deep appreciation for the creativity and dedication required to perfect one's musical skills. While I'm not musical, witnessing his exhilaration while playing the drums inspired me to find my own passions, such as tennis and writing, which provide a similar sense of endorphin release and help me keep my mental health in check.

MAKE TIME SERVE YOU

At one time in my life, I thought I couldn't afford to give of my time. Now I can't afford not to. The workouts and the camaraderie and the connections are far too beneficial to my mental and physical health.

The difference between those who succeed and those who fail is that those who make it never give up. And I might add, those who succeed often stay busier and more active than those who fail.

My father was not one to waste time sleeping. Even if we arrived at our home office at 8:10 a.m., he would exclaim, "Good afternoon, half the day is gone!" He had little patience for laziness and strongly believed in tackling the most challenging tasks first. He often quoted the phrase, "Sleep when you're dead."

My father spent any free time he did have reading or watching the news, seldom indulging in entertainment television, as he found little educational value in the fictitious lives portrayed. However, he made an exception for his favorite movie, *The Bridge on the River Kwai,* which won seven Academy Awards in 1957. The film depicted British prisoners of war constructing a bridge for their Japanese captors, highlighting the importance of never losing sight of the mission at hand. My father valued education and knowledge and believed that being armed with knowledge was the best arsenal one could have.

If I go for a walk, I use it as an opportunity to listen to an educational book on tape. While driving to an appointment, I may tune in to an informational podcast.

Our family once employed a man formerly incarcerated. He explained that when he arrived at San Quentin State Penitentiary in San Francisco, he read a sign, "Don't serve time, let time serve you." He went in with that message in mind and got a degree, which his previous criminal lifestyle had not allowed. He got fit and became a role model for other prisoners.

After her brother died, I took my mother to a grief counseling group at my children's school church. Sitting in the dimly lit vestibule, we met other grief-stricken participants and heard their stories. One gay man had lost his lover, leading his family to discover his sexuality. They were neither accepting nor understanding and they cut him off—doubling his grief. Another woman discovered her husband was having an affair after she'd intercepted the lover's emails. Story after intimate story was shared within our group. Then an elderly man, evidence of a life full of harsh and sad years etched on a face so creased he resembled a Shar-Pei dog. When he shared that his wife of 64 years had passed away, the group moaned in sympathetic unison until he exclaimed, "And I'm so glad the goddamned bitch is gone!" Everyone else seemed to lean in with compassion, and I was the only one to laugh aloud. To me it was inconceivable that he would make such a statement. As I gathered my wits and tried to overcome my embarrassment that no one else found his comment not only outrageous, but humorous, I summoned all my big-girl courage to speak up.

"If you're so glad she's gone, why are you here for grief counseling?" I asked.

"I'm mourning the fact I wasted 64 years," he said.

Let that sink in. This old curmudgeon was seeking group grief counseling for the years he felt had been stolen. At some point, he said he felt like he had died, even though his heart continued to beat.

Another elderly woman in the group, who was attending to help her cope with a terminal diagnosis, said, "The only regret you'll hear from an old person in a nursing home is the time they didn't, and they wish they had."

That day, the grief counselor gave us an assignment to write a letter to ourselves, put it in the mail, and to paste a note on the front of the envelope not to open it for one year. In the letter, we were to describe our current pain and where we hoped to be when we read the letter in 365 days.

In my letter, I vowed that I would not mourn a day of my life. I wrote that letter to myself over 22 years ago, and I still revisit it as a reminder. I decided after hearing the elderly, angry old man's share that I would make every day a get-up-and-get-on-it day!

My hope is that you will too.

The average life expectancy in the US, as of 2023, is 76 years (Harvard T.H. Chan School of Public Health, 2023), which is about 27,375 days.

Make each of them count. And don't let yourself wind up regretting what you didn't do when you had the chance. The clock is ticking.

You will face naysayers, people who doubt your capacity for success, your will and determination. There will be distractions and sacrifices as people try to dissuade you from following the source of your motivation. They may shun you, and you may be surprised by the lack of support and enthusiasm as you embark on your journey to build generational wealth.

I love the Winston Churchill quote, "If you are going through Hell, keep on going."

The best is yet to be. Now get up and get on it!

GET UP AND GET ON IT

- Don't serve time, let time serve you.
- Embrace a life of purpose and resilience.
- Remember that having it all is a matter of choice: make your choice!
- Pay attention to others whom you perceive as "having it all." How busy are they? What are their habits? What can you learn from them and adopt in your own life?

12

PAY IT FORWARD

There was a moment in your life when a door opened and let
your future in

You may have been struggling and defeated and didn't know
where to begin

But, someone paid it forward, their knowledge, time, talents and resources
they bestowed

Your life forever changed by the gifts their grace and generosity flowed

So, pay it forward, and be a part of another's history

Success takes a village; there is no problem to solve or mystery

Take a chance on someone, go ahead and roll the dice

The return on paying it forward doesn't come with a price

The interest is tangible as you watch your efforts improve someone's existence

So be a part and lift up others and watch them go the distance

—Dana Frank

Y ou cannot receive with a closed fist. It's one of the most valuable lessons I learned from a family of mentors who have
taught me, by example, the value of hard work, finding success,
giving back, and paying it forward. My mother's siblings include
the first Black flight attendant Alaska Airlines would hire and retire,
Mardra Jones Jay, and Federal Judge Richard A. Jones, who has
overseen some of Seattle's most notorious cases. But most famous is
my mother's brother, my uncle, music impresario, Emmy, Grammy,
Oscar, and Tony Award winner (EGOT), the legendary Quincy
Jones. From their extremely humble beginnings, being raised by
my grandmother, a lifelong domestic worker, and my grandfather,
a carpenter, they have all been exemplary examples of what it means
to give back. The awards, honors, and scholarships that they have
funded, and the hours of volunteer service, both domestically and
internationally, have impacted and changed the lives of many and
the world for the better. And they have taught me much.

But my most impactful lessons started at home.

Giving Thanks and Giving, Thanks

For some the holidays can be a tough time. Missing loved ones
and feeling overindulged by the warmth and love surrounding
our homes, it is hard not to feel guilty when so much happiness is amplified, knowing so many are suffering. Our family
Thanksgiving was not an exception, and it was always a favorite
holiday in our house. Mama would start grocery shopping a week
before the big day. She had to get to Safeway, our local grocery
store, before they ran out of Dromedary corn bread mix for her
homemade stuffing and grab the cans of Aunt Penny's white sauce
before they sold out, as she would not accept any substitutions.
The stuffing alone is a labor of love as over the years I have watched
Mama cook down the onions, bell peppers, cornbread, and sea-
sonings sautéing over the hot stove and with a strong muscle grip

to mix the ingredients just right, so it didn't burn. I watched as Mama took the turkey parts and boiled them to make the gravy separately. The yams, homemade mac n' cheese, candied yams, string beans, ham, sweet potato pies, and rum pound cake make my mouth water just reminiscing.

We had made our donations to the local missions. How could we enjoy such an amazing feast knowing that less than a mile away, so many people were suffering because they did not have shelter, let alone a hearty meal to enjoy with loved ones? My siblings drove to skid row, our impoverished downtrodden segment of downtown Seattle. There they deposited bags of prepared dinners into the hands of the needy, along with turkey and all the fixings, to nourish those they encountered who were down and out.

After our charitable service, we prepared to set the table for a guilt-free day of thanks, when out of nowhere, Daddy entered the house with a stranger. This unkempt man smelled of the filthy streets he had been living on.

I was baffled as the time was approaching 4 p.m., which was when my day of fasting would cease and I could indulge in Mama's soulful meal. Was Daddy trying to rent this man an apartment? On Thanksgiving? Right at dinner time? Was he there to seek employment? What was this about? When and where did Daddy find this vagrant? But my biggest question was, why now? Wasn't it time to celebrate and give thanks for all our blessings? Hadn't we done enough donating to the local churches, and my sisters delivering food to the needy?

"Gerald, dinner is being served," Mama said, annoyed.

"Family, this is Norman. He will be joining us for dinner tonight."

Daddy excused himself and took Norman to the guest bathroom for a piping hot shower. When Norman was done, Daddy sat Norman down and gave him a much-needed shave and hair trim.

We made a place setting for Norman, and he enjoyed what I am certain was the best meal of his life.

Daddy often shared stories of growing up in Detroit, and how everyone looked after each other. If you needed shelter, food, a loan, or support, the community became your extended family. Daddy's door was always open. Often it was a revolving cycle of those interested in understanding his success and finding the trajectory to create their own.

People would stop by morning, noon, and night to seek his guidance, counsel, and insights. Often it felt like an invasion of privacy because there were no boundaries as far as Daddy was concerned. One of his favorite sayings was, "A sucker without heart may as well be dead."

Selflessness

My father also taught me that sometimes supporting a cause, especially the ones involving speaking out against injustice, is more important than avoiding the discomfort it will bring. He taught me that being an advocate often means getting out of my comfort zone. As Dr. Martin Luther King, Jr. wrote, "Our lives begin to end the day we become silent about things that matter."

Such was the case when I was around 20 years old and summoned by my father to his office.

"You heard me. Community activists, Charlie James and Earl Debnam are sleeping up in the old Colman School to claim the building for an African American Museum," my father repeated.

The Colman School in Seattle was the first school in the area attended by Black students, and it had hired many Black teachers. When it was closed in 1985 by the Seattle School District, many felt it should become a Black history museum. There were approximately 40 Black activists occupying the property, which had no heat and no running water.

Daddy continued, "We gotta support those brothers. It's cold in there, and they need some nourishment."

"So, you expect me to go make sandwiches and take them up there?" I balked.

"Something wrong with your hearing, suddenly?"

"Daddy, can't you just order pizza delivery?"

"Dana, they need to know they got the community support, and I want them to know you put heart into your efforts."

I made my way to the kitchen and slapped some lunch meat on whole wheat bread, smearing mayonnaise, adding a slice of cheese and tomatoes, all of which I detested, and deposited my pathetic offerings into plastic baggies. When I was done with the preparations, I re-entered the office where my father and sister were in deep conversation.

"Dana's Delivery," I said as I held up the paper bag. "Let's go."

Daddy turned in his chair to face me. "Go on now, you're a big girl. Take this to those men and tell them Gerald Frank and family said to keep fighting."

"I'm not going up there by myself!" I shrieked.

Moments later, I pulled my car into the abandoned parking lot of Colman School. I cursed my father aloud as I marched across the crunchy gravel. *Why can't he deliver this food his own damn self?* I thought as I reached the entry with bolted locks. I peered through the old schoolhouse and didn't see any signs of life. Dust was settling in as I fumed over my options. I knocked, but my knuckles pounding on the door were barely audible. I wasn't willing to investigate and exhaust myself with efforts to attract attention. I heard a vehicle approaching and turned to see a KING 5 television truck. I quickly deposited the bag of sandwiches at the front door and rushed to my car.

Fast forward to today, and the Northwest African American Museum (NWAAM) sits on this site. NWAAM is a positive presence in the community and had the fight not begun, this treasured piece of our Pacific Northwest history would not exist.

As a child, I watched as our home office was a revolving door for people seeking my father's knowledge and expertise. My father was always open to teaching and paying forward lessons to help others achieve economic freedom. My eldest sister's first marriage didn't last (neither did her second but who's counting); however, her ex learned early from my father's training on the power of investing. Today, 50 years later, my sister's ex has built a thriving rental business in the Central District, which his daughter is now taking over. Daily I hear stories of the impact that my father had on others' careers and how his influence changed the trajectory of lives. Kenneth Lombard, president and CEO of Bridge Housing and co-founder of Johnson Development Company, an organization focused on retail development in urban communities, shared how, as a young impressionable Black man, he called on my father one day and asked to shadow him. Daddy said, "Sure, son, be at my house at 6:00 a.m. and not a moment later, and we will take a ride." Sure enough, when Ken arrived at 5:59 a.m., my father was warming up his truck, and they drove all over the city as Daddy shared his insights on investing.

Another classic example of the impact my father had was shared by former Seattle Super Sonic, author, and entrepreneur, Dean Tolson. Dean was born into poverty in Kansas to a single mother and spent many years in the foster care system. Dean is 6'8" and athletically talented, and he was focused on one goal and that was playing basketball. He was passed through the education system and graduated nearly illiterate, with what he compares to a third-grade education. Because of Dean's lack of literacy basics, he holds the record as one of the lowest paid NBA players in history with a take-home of a few hundred dollars a week. My father mentored Dean and showed by example what a successful Black man could create if he put the effort forward. Dean returned to school and graduated magna cum laude with a master's degree in education. Dean started a successful carpet cleaning business in Seattle and earned a million-dollar contract with Boeing. Dean is another example of someone who did not allow the circumstances of his birth to define his destiny.

MY FAMILY OF ROLE MODELS

I look to my uncle, Richard A. Jones, who started off as a King County prosecuting attorney and then private practice at the major law firm Bogel & Gates before he became assistant US attorney. I know the stories of the racism he fought to reach the bench where he presided over high-profile cases, including the prosecution of Gary Ridgway, the notorious Green River Killer, who is known to have killed nearly 50 women in our state. Jones's work for advancing minorities in education, law, and as a mentor to minority youth in Seattle and his record of working to level the playing field in diversity and fairness are beyond reproach.

My Aunt Margie was one of the first Black flight attendants that Alaska Airlines would hire and celebrated her retirement after 20 years of service. I will never forget the day of her final landing: coworkers lined the runway dressed in the signature Alaska outfits they wore over those decades. In 1964, my aunt was working at the gas company. Affirmative action was urging African Americans to seek employment in jobs previously held only by Whites. That journey took my aunt to India, Russia, Europe, and Asia, the Holy Land, and the Middle East. My aunt has always had compassion for those marginalized in all arenas of life. She and her husband, my Uncle Chris, fund scholarships and support children worldwide in need.

My Aunt Barbara Despenza spent her career working as regional director of unemployment insurance programs for the 10 Midwest states of Illinois, Indiana, Michigan, Minnesota, Ohio, Wisconsin, Missouri, Iowa, Nebraska, and Kansas, where she oversaw the administration of nearly $20 billion in annual benefits. She spends her retirement teaching senior citizens computer skills.

Uncle Boo, the nickname my sister gave Mama's older brother Waymond because he kept all of us in line, had the most dedicated work ethic in our family. He would show up at our family home, and his presence would be announced by the sound of him using the leaf-blower to clear the yard of leaves and debris. The man was constantly in motion. He kept his car in impeccable condition. He was never without employment and saw most other people as lazy. In his mind, there was always work to do. And he was insanely in shape. We jokingly called him our Black Jack LaLanne, the fitness and nutrition guru who passed away at the age of 96. Uncle Boo worked out daily, be it jogging, running, or biking. He lived a clean lifestyle and shunned alcohol and smoking, so when he got cancer and died within a week after surgery at age 71, we were beyond consoling.

The remarkable reality is that when I reflect on these gifted, strong, industrious individuals like my late uncle Lloyd was fortunate to be mentored by, they were and are resilient and successful through times when this was no easy feat. Each of them faced insurmountable challenges, dysfunction, racism, rejection, and life struggles; however, they were able to rise above, be homeowners and productive members of society, giving back. My aunt Catherine instead of some took in foster children. Aunt Janet tended to the elderly. Some adopted children who had been abandoned by birth parents struggling with circumstances and unable to cope. In our family, we don't look at blood as the requirement to be family. We look at family as individuals who carry the same history and torch to make a legacy.

Impacting Others, Big and Small

The legacy of Gary Veloric, whom you met earlier in the Achieving It All chapter, is not defined by seeking admiration or attention. Instead, he believes in letting his actions speak for themselves. Alongside his business endeavors, he channels his energy into supporting charitable causes.

He initiated an entrepreneur program at his alma mater, American University the Veloric Center for Entrepreneurship, which will equip students with essential skills for succeeding in business. Scheduled to launch in the fall of 2023, this degree program will include business competitions and cover fundamental aspects like pitch deck creation and management. In fact, he supports numerous charitable organizations, with MusiCares, where he has served on the board of directors, being particularly close to his heart.

Having personally witnessed the impact of MusiCares on the lives of musicians facing financial or mental health challenges, Gary is dedicated to giving back to the community.

While his accomplishments may not always be in the spotlight, Gary's mark can be seen in the lives he has touched, the businesses he has transformed, and the charitable causes he supports. His story serves as an inspiration for aspiring entrepreneurs and highlights the importance of combining business acumen with a creative spirit.

As Gary's journey continues to unfold, one thing remains certain: his legacy will be defined not only by his achievements but also by the positive impact he leaves behind in the lives of others.

When I asked Donald Thompson what he wanted his legacy to be, he said, "Helping others be their best." With that humble goal in mind, Donald and his wife give all their salaries to their charitable causes. They have college scholarship programs domestically, and they support Untold.org, a mission in Africa that helps women who have life-threatening diseases like AIDS and their children find work and thrive.

MY JOYS OF GIVING

I learned lessons early on in compassion and as the saying goes, "You have never really lived until you have done something for someone who can't repay you." Not only do you reap the feel-good reward of knowing you are doing good, but I can also attest the benefits of my connections through my outreach are magnified in comparison to what I give.

Every day I look for opportunities to pay it forward. A smile truly is contagious.

Dana Frank presenting MoPop Founders Award to her uncle, Quincy Jones

In March 2022, I had the privilege of honoring the work of my Uncle Quincy by presenting him with the Founders Award of Seattle's Museum of Popular Culture, or MoPop. I serve on the board of directors for the museum, which was founded by Microsoft co-founder Paul Allen. MoPop's mission is to make creative expression a life-changing force by offering experiences that inspire and connect our communities. Our under-21 music showcase, Sound Off, connects young musicians with the tools and resources to level up their career and future.

The communities I support through my service on the board of MoPop, serving on the advisory board for Treehouse for Foster Kids, and teaching tennis to homeless middle schoolers are predominantly Black and from marginalized homes. I have mentored these young people to challenge the belief that their limitations *are* indeed limitations. I encourage them to believe that they too can build a life they desire and create an income that is not paycheck to paycheck. They do not have to remain a victim of their circumstances or their parents' poor decisions.

I serve on public boards, am a member of International Women's Groups, private social clubs, teach tennis to homeless middle school students, and I have hosted an annual holiday drive for the past 20 years for foster children. Some of my best connections, friendships, and business relationships have been born of these volunteer opportunities and organizations. I believe that our children are our future, and they did not ask to come here. Therefore, we owe them. (When we see the statistics that tell us African American men make up 40% of the incarcerated population but are only 13% of the population, it is our duty to step in and be their village.)

MY CALL TO YOU

There are always opportunities to be a part of your communities. When was the last time you volunteered at a homeless shelter? When have you donated clothes to your local Dress for Success? How about a time you did a holiday drive for needy children? Perhaps you spend your hours after school tutoring children with learning disabilities. Think about how rewarding it felt, knowing that for a moment, a day, or a lifetime, your actions have made an impact.

Or do you watch the horrific headlines and news stories where tornados, floods, earthquakes, and natural disasters have destroyed another community, and your heart bleeds for their misfortune, but you don't take the time to donate because you will leave it to the others. There are no others. It's you. And giving back or paying it forward doesn't have to cost money. There are numerous opportunities that don't cost any money where you can pay it forward and change the trajectory of someone's future.

Pay it forward. Whenever you see an opportunity, it is what we are called to do and that is lift another up.

To whom much is given, much is required.

My hope in sharing my journey is that we create action on a long overdue conversation that you don't get in a classroom.

There is not much I have not experienced, including family estrangement, death of loved ones, divorce, the destructive power of drugs and alcohol, discrimination, and financial hardship. I also know the payoff of hard work, the fight to rise from the trenches, the necessity of compassion and giving back, and the blessing of working for myself and with those I love the most.

GET UP AND GET ON IT!

- Every day, look for the opportunity to lift someone up. Whether you choose to give your money, time, talent, advice, or connections, there is always an opportunity to help change the narrative of someone else's future.

- Try it: smile at a stranger, and I guarantee you it will be returned. Be intentional on certain days and set out to offer random acts of kindness. Buy the person behind you in line in Starbucks their latte. Take the time to listen to someone's story.

- Seek out those who may benefit from your skills. You can lend your skills and talents to various organizations to help those who otherwise would not have the opportunity.

- Despite whatever hardships you are facing, find a role model and observe his or her behavior of giving. And then do what that person does.

- Paying it forward means speaking up against injustice. Be a community advocate.

- Teach your children early—by modeling with your own actions—the value in the act of selflessness.

13

MASTER OF MY FATE

The best life lessons are earned not bought
In school or on the job, pay attention to what's taught
As students we're told to absorb in all our classes
To avoid the poor decisions made by the masses
For detours you'll pay the price and feel the wrath
When you face the Y in the road, remember, you chose the path
We use our diplomas, degrees, and real life choices
Success is found listening and acting on our own internal voices
When the student becomes the teacher, it's time to graduate
To thank those who came before and to become the master of my fate.

—Dana Frank

I grew up reading and writing poetry. One of my favorite poems was, "Children Learn What They Live" by Dorothy Law Nolte.

The significance of Law Nolte's wise words was the reminder that children often become what they are exposed to. Meaning, as children, we mimic the behavior we witness from the significant adults in our life. This can be a negative influence or a positive one. My husband, for example, was raised by a librarian. He spent countless days with his mother classifying books through the Dewey Decimal system. He never lost the joy of reading and to this day, he has three or four books going at a time.

Based on my upbringing, the chances were that I'd bring forward into adulthood much more trouble than I have. My father's actions and behaviors meant my childhood was chaotic. I was not the beneficiary of a traditional nurturing and stable environment.

Yet I was somehow able to navigate through the uncertain terrain. I took every one of his putdowns as a challenge as I bided my time until I could become independent. I developed and held onto my own values, even when my father was angry that they did not align with his poor choices and judgment.

My coping mechanism was not to argue with him, as my sisters and mother would, but I would bottle up my rage. I would ignore his demands if I did not agree, but I would not voice my objections. It took a greater toll on me physically and mentally than I realized. Although my father did not believe in therapy and said it was for the weak minded, in my 20s and throughout my adult life, I found this avenue a helpful resource for coming to terms with his abuse, addictions, and failures. Did I doubt myself and my capabilities? Absolutely. I had to find my voice which had been silenced by my role as the youngest and the peacekeeper.

I keep a magnet on my refrigerator which was a gift from one of my life coaches. The message, titled "The Most Beautiful People," is written by Elizabeth Kubler-Ross, a Swiss-American psychiatrist and pioneer on death studies. She writes that beautiful people have known adversity, defeat, struggles, and suffering and yet have managed to emerge from the depths with compassion and loving concern.

Many people have asked me if I have Stockholm Syndrome, as it seems unusual for me not to harbor any resentment toward my father. I came to accept that he operated based on his own struggles and personal demons, which included battles with alcohol and drugs. Later I discovered that he had been diagnosed with bipolar disorder, a mental illness characterized by alternating periods of depression and excessively elevated mood. I chose to embrace the lessons I learned from him during his stable moments and to disengage from and not fuel his manic episodes.

Still, some days I found the insults, embarrassment, and outbursts to be unbearable. His reckless financial decisions jeopardized our security, and my mother, sisters, and I often became enablers in our efforts to protect him and our family business.

It is said that there is a fine line between love and hate. While I despised the difficult years, I loved my father because he was my greatest teacher. To this day, I continue to live by his vision with respect to changing the narrative. Not accepting the hand you have been dealt by the circumstances of your birth has been a powerful motivator.

I cherish the memories of our banter and miss our conversations about life and finance. If he were alive today, I know he would beam with pride to witness how his seemingly improbable decision of buying that first investment at the age of eighteen has transformed into something extraordinary.

I have allowed my tenacity and accomplishments to speak for themselves. Just as my father could never have imagined the life he created, I am certain that if he saw me sitting in a board meeting with two other Black women—MoPop's CEO, Michele Y. Smith, and Shaunta Hyde, an Amazon executive and Fortune 100 business leader—he would place his hand on his chest and say, "That's my stuff." In his wildest dreams, he would never have imagined that his youngest daughter would fly by private plane to Blackberry Farms, Tennessee. I have carried the torch that he ignited seventy years ago, and now I pass it on to his grandchildren so that their great-grandchildren will have their own stories to tell.

My father may have held outdated beliefs and engaged in hurtful behavior, but I choose to remember him for the constructive lessons he taught me when he was in a stable state of mind. Despite his flaws, he instilled in me a drive to defy expectations and to strive for success. He may not have understood or supported my pursuits as a woman, but his influence fueled my determination to prove him wrong.

Over the years, I have worked hard to build my own path, guided by the values and principles that I hold dear. Along the way, I have defied stereotypes and shattered glass ceilings. As I sit in board meetings and collaborate with other powerful women leaders, I carry with me the legacy of my father's unlikely investment in what he taught me.

But it's not just about my personal achievements. I am committed to using my success as a platform for change. I strive to create opportunities for others who face barriers and to challenge the systems that perpetuate inequality. I know that my father, in his own complicated way, wanted the best for his daughters.

And now it is my responsibility to continue his legacy by advocating for gender equality and empowering the next generation.

In my journey, I have come to understand that love and forgiveness can coexist alongside acknowledging past pain. I have made peace with the fact that my father was flawed, just like any and every human being. His struggles with mental illness, his chauvinistic views, and his addictive tendencies were all part of a complex individual who was both a captor and a mentor.

While I cannot change the past, I can shape the future. I can choose to break free from the cycle of enabling and protectiveness that plagued our family for so long. I can raise my voice against injustice and work toward creating a world where gender does not limit one's potential.

So, as I carry forward the torch that my father ignited, I do so with a sense of purpose and a commitment to making a difference. I am grateful for the lessons he taught me, even in the most challenging of times. And as I look to the future, I am determined to leave a lasting impact, not just for myself but for generations to come.

GET UP AND GET ON IT!

- If you are a parent or frequently interact with young children, it's important to realize that your behavior, whether active or passive, serves as a model that will shape their lives indefinitely. Even if you were raised in a tumultuous environment, it's crucial not to let the pain and suffering define you or hinder your pursuit of success.

- Adhere to your own set of morals and values, holding yourself accountable to them and living by their principles.

- Maintain a clear focus on your aspirations and ambitions. Utilize imaginative visualization techniques, put your goals in writing, keep a journal, and create vision boards to reinforce your vision.

- Recognize that forgiveness is a precious gift you give yourself, freeing yourself from the burdens of resentment and enabling personal growth.

EPILOGUE: YOU CAN'T TAKE IT WITH YOU

"**D**addy, it's me," my voice called out as I entered the toasty hospital room. My father stood before me wearing his velour robe and applejack leather cap. Behind his dark glasses, I imagined what had consumed his thoughts.

He had been a survivor. An 18-year-old Black man born 66 years after slavery ended. A musician and a businessman, he had changed the trajectory of not only his life but generations to follow. He had survived heart attacks, kidney failure, a divorce, business on the brink of bankruptcy, and a system that was designed to hold him back.

"What are you doing?" I asked, taking a seat on his bed.

"Sugar, it's so good to see you." He greeted me with a kiss to my forehead. He patted my stomach. "So how are you feeling carrying my grandson?"

"Daddy, you don't know it's a boy. I told you I wouldn't peek at the ultrasound."

He shrugged. "I know. But that's a man-child. I just hope I can be here to see him."

"Why are you talking like that? I read you the letter from Dr. Wollack. He said much to his surprise, the committee said they'd be willing to consider you for a heart and kidney transplant."

My father squeezed my hand as he slowly crawled into bed. "Dana, I appreciate your optimism. But there comes a time when you must deal with reality. So, let's talk. Time may be running out, and I don't want to leave you with any questions. Ask me anything you want to know."

I smiled demurely. "Anything?"

He nodded. "Anything."

"What drove you to fight and survive as you did?"

He smiled. "I didn't have a choice. Sink or swim were my only options. I believe people get lazy, so avoid that personality type. When you see opportunity and people building, it is contagious. Those are the ones who will drive your success in life."

I sprawled sideways on my father's bed and looked at him intently. I was 7 months pregnant, and my baby was actively moving. I took my hand and gently rubbed my stomach. "You protect this property, and it will take care of you and my grandchildren to come," he quoted.

"Hear me out, I'm trusting you. I know I raised you to continue the fight. It *has* been my sweat and now your equity."

I watched his lethargic body and heard the shortness of breath as he reached for the oxygen tubes by his bedside. The cruelest of all fates, I reasoned, was that his mind was still active. I turned and faced him, suddenly unashamed by my tears. I tried to commit his face and our conversation to memory.

"Sugar, I don't want you getting emotional now," my father said. "This is just life's reality. Don't let a day pass when you feel sorry for your daddy. I've done it all, had a good life, everything I've ever dreamed of accomplishing and more. It's time to pass the baton."

I squeezed my father's hand. I wanted to respond, but my voice was gone.

He nodded as if he understood. "We've been on a turbulent ride, but your daddy never backed down. I know things weren't always easy on you, your mama, and sisters." He chuckled. "But I did put some *fun* in *dysfunctional*."

I smiled just as my father's home health nurse knocked at the bedroom door.

"Hi, Simeon, come on in," I said.

Simeon nodded at me. He was a man of few words. Simeon had been in home health care for 15 years, and he was skilled in assisting end-stage heart-disease patients.

"Mr. Frank, it's time for your dialysis," Simeon said. He walked to the microwave and inserted the fluid-filled packet.

"I'd better get going." I rose. "We can finish this conversation later."

"Baby, just sit and let me look at you. I don't know how much longer I'll be able to do that."

"Dad, you have to stop being so pessimistic. Tomorrow, you go in for vascular studies and a right heart cauterization so we can move forward with the transplants. Think about the people that we met in the support groups. It's gonna happen." I kissed his cheek, "And you're gonna be here to see your grandbaby. But in the meantime, rest."

"Hey, sugar," my father called as I reached the door to leave.

I stopped. "Yeah, Dad."

"I don't want you to think I'm throwing in the towel or nothin'. I mean, it ain't over till the fat lady dances, right?"

"She sings, Dad! It ain't over till the fat lady sings."

My father balled his fist and saluted me with the Black Power sign.

I smiled and gave a thumbs-up signal as I exited the room. I couldn't see his eyes, but I imagined the twinkle behind his glasses. And then, I could hear my father mumble as I headed down the steps, "It ain't over till the fat lady sings."

When my father was diagnosed with congestive heart failure, he was still in his 50s and young by life standards. He was angry that his body was failing him. He was bitter at the oxygen tank that became his constant companion. His drinking began to escalate as he tried to escape the misery. Many times, he called my home at 2 or 3 a.m., summoning me to get down to his house because the Fire Department was en route because he was having a heart attack. When I arrived to find him fine, the Fire Department emergency responders checking him over, he'd have me write a check to The Firemen's Fund. I discovered these calls were not a medical emergency, however, but his own fear of sleeping and that he might not awake.

On his last Christmas, I took him to the mall and wheeled him around to enjoy the sights and sounds of the season. A former tenant approached us. She bent down to my father and said, "Hey, aren't you Gerald Frank?"

He barely lifted his head and replied, "I used to be."

He was defeated. Remember that he believed that humans only used 10% of their brain, so he thought he should be able to summon his mental strength to overcome his fragile state. This effort failed along with his kidneys. His ankles swelled up like fat socks resting on his feet.

I asked him if he was afraid, and although I knew the answer, he feigned toughness and said no. I was able to get him into a group therapy with other family groups facing the end of their lives. The group sessions and support of other individuals reflecting on life and their legacies eased my father's anxiety.

For a time, Daddy kept hope alive that he would get a heart transplant or a miracle that would restore his health. But in the end, he accepted that he was on death row without a chance of an appeal. He survived long enough to witness the birth of his grandson, Brett, a curly-headed precocious tyke, and to enjoy the first few years of the child's life. Although he never met his granddaughter, Taryn and Brett have reaped the benefits of what their grandfather started 70 years ago.

Gerald Frank exceeded his medical expectations. On his final night alive, July 6, 1996, I gave him permission to go. I told him his work was done and that his legacy will live on. He was terminated from the transplant list after disconnecting himself from the heart monitor, checking out at 2:00 a.m., and taking a taxi home.

The journey has been filled with challenges, but the rewards and fulfillment gained along the way make every hurdle worth overcoming.

And that is legacy.

"These trees which he or she plants, and under whose shade he or she shall never sit, for the sake of his or her children and his or her children's children. . ." —Author unknown.

ACKNOWLEDGMENTS

Mama, I can't count how many times you have smiled and shrugged and said, "I did my best, that behavior is from your father's side." I am beyond blessed, as I inherited the best of both of you: Daddy's grit and your grace. You have been my best friend, partner, confidant, and champion, and taught me unconditional love. You also taught me to wear my Spanx, the outfit that's appropriate for every occasion, how to *get down* in the kitchen, and to keep my independence, both mentally and financially. You've earned many nicknames: Sister Mary Sanitary, for your commitment to cleanliness; and Tutu (grandmother), as you are the wise elder to all. From your birthname, Willie, to when your parochial grade-school teachers thought that was meant for a boy and changed it to Theresa, you've been known by many names, but none more important than my mama. Your years of modeling are reflected not only in your timeless beauty and wisdom, but you've also been modeling what it means to be compassionate and generous but not to suffer fools. When I reflect on our journey, it feels inadequate to say, "Thank you" for always believing in me and us but *thank you*. I'm eternally grateful. I couldn't love you more if I wanted to.

I couldn't have done any of this without my late father, Gerald Frank. I carried your last name as I was the son you never had and your last born. I also carry your last name because I am proud to be your daughter. The vision that changed the narrative for our family's story began from behind your glasses. How I marvel at your tenacity, grit, and never-give-in-or-out life motto. The gratitude I have for "Daddy's lessons and blessin's" I carry every day, and that is legacy. Were there tough days? Absolutely. But you did manage to put the *fun* in *dysfunctional*, and those were some of my best life lessons and memories. There is not a day that goes by when I don't ask myself, "What would Daddy do?" Thank you for the navigation and for showing me that guardian angels are real. I miss you madly, Daddy; however, you are such a part of who I am that you are still with me every day when I get up and get on it. I love you to infinity.

For my children, Brett and Taryn, you both have always made me beyond proud. You each took top awards in your respective classes. You have excelled not only academically, but also athletically and in every aspect of life. Though you have gone through such pain with the untimely tragic loss of your father, Steve, your resilience, and your dedication to our family and doing good for others is remarkable. Daily I am overwhelmed by how you have become my teachers. Lessons in compassion, love, hard work, and your belief in our family are reminders of how fortunate I am to be mother to each of you. You have each earned the right to carry the baton for what your grandparents created more than 70 years ago. You both make me beam with pride, and to have given birth to you is to know love. I entrust your grandparents' vision in your hands and for your children's children.

A special note of gratitude for my son, Brett. It was because of your insistence, passion, and belief in me that this book and the story of our journey is being shared. I am eternally grateful. I know we say, "If it's not one thing, it's your mother." Admittedly, I'm not your traditional Mama, so thank you for your patience and being my right hand.

For my husband, Eric. Thank you for being the best critic, even when I'm an "askhole" and ask your opinion but do my own thing. I'm so grateful you grew up with a librarian and thus for your wisdom, guidance, and editing skills. Thank you for sharing this wonderful life of ours and for being the most dependable partner a girl could ask for.

Thank you to my brand strategist, Charlie Fusco, for your brilliant guidance and believing in me to take on this project from the beginning.

Thank you to Chris Flett, my Ghost CEO, who makes me laugh and simultaneously teaches me to not make excuses or give them.

Boni Wagner-Stafford, my editor and miracle worker, I am blown away at how you get me. Your talent in taking my writings and thoughts and making it a cohesive, flowing book that will help generations to follow is a testament to your talent and expertise. I am forever grateful.

To my DE, Kristi Bennett, thank you for loving and encouraging my poetry.

Thanks to my sisters by birth and by choice, Tracie and Patti, for rooting me on, critiquing, and caring. Your input and insights have been incomparable. My love for you runs deep.

Tracie, my sister. You're a gifted writer, author, blogger, trend setter, and advocate for all, and right from childhood you set the bar high. Thank you for helping me block out the nonsense. I credit you with many sayings, including, "Stay in your lane; there's less traffic." The Delaney Sisters forever.

To Daymond John. When we met, I asked you for three things:

1. Let's not let this be our first and last meeting.
2. Please consider writing my foreword if you felt my book worthy.
3. Please share some of your game-changer-ness with me and help me amplify my story.

You answered an emphatic *yes* to all. You have proven that what we all see on television is the real deal. You are "The People's Shark." Thank you for your compassion, empathy, and for sharing your wealth of knowledge. You are a game changer.

It is true when they say it takes a village. I will not even attempt to thank every member of my tribe who has supported me in this journey. You know who you are, and you inspire me daily. I am better because of you. I hope through these pages I can support you on your journey to understanding the importance of changing the trajectory of not only your future, but the next generation to come.

Let every venture be an adventure!

Xoxo

Dana

ABOUT THE AUTHOR

Dana Frank is one of Seattle's most celebrated real estate investors who has beaten the odds as an owner/operator of a business founded by her parents more than 70 years ago. She has been an active board member of the Museum of Popular Culture (MoPop) for the past 9 years and, last year, co-chaired its signature Founders Award fundraiser to honor her uncle, music impresario Quincy Jones.

In 1950, Frank's parents were "Black and broke—but not broken." Growing up in her family-run apartment rental business that her father started when he was just 18 years old, she was surrounded by the erratic situations caused by renters, intense police interventions, and a constant struggle to secure financing only afforded to White businessmen. While her father's unconventional business practices helped him amass a sizable real estate empire, after 32 years, Frank and her mother broke away from her father's financial protection and opposing business strategies to set out on their own.

Today, Frank sits at the helm of her own family real estate empire to create generational legacy, working with her 90-year-old mother and adult children. She continues to champion political change in banking laws and is passionate about educating others on the power of investing and how real estate ownership can change the trajectory of current and future generations.

In 2023, Frank pioneered the creation of the annual National Black Families in Business Day, to honor and encourage all Black families in business, which will be celebrated annually on August 26. Along with her sister, Tracie, she also hosts a popular blog entitled www.Menopausebarbees.com that celebrates women.

Frank donates much of her time to those less fortunate. She is often seen at fundraisers throughout the Puget Sound region. She is frequently called upon, due to her infectious personality, to do "The Ask" at live charity events, including an annual gift drive she founded for Treehouse for Foster Kids, now in its 20th year. She teaches tennis at Nativity School, which supports homeless children, and supports Mary's Place, whose mission is "no one's child should sleep outside," as well as many other charities.

Today, Frank splits her time, with her husband, Eric, between Nashville, Scottsdale, and her hometown of Seattle. She has two children—a son, Brett, who is now her protégé and business partner, and a daughter, Taryn, who recently graduated from Chapman University with a degree in marketing while getting her real estate license. When not otherwise engaged, Frank enjoys traveling, playing tennis, attending sporting events, reading, and watching movies.

REFERENCES

Aladangady, A. and Forde, A. (2021). *Wealth inequality and the racial wealth gap* [online]. www.federalreserve.gov. Available at: https://www.federalreserve.gov/econres/notes/feds-notes/wealth-inequality-and-the-racial-wealth-gap-20211022.html#:~:text=In%20the%20United%20States%2C%20the.

Annie E. Casey Foundation (2022). *Child well-being in single-parent families* [online]. Available at: https://www.aecf.org/blog/child-well-being-in-single-parent-families.

April S. (n.d.). *7 companies like divvy homes (Alternatives) for rent-to-own in 2023* [online]. Epic Home Ideas. Available at: https://www.epichomeideas.com/companies-like-divvy-homes/ [Accessed 10 Jul. 2023].

Associated Press. (2023). *DOJ announces a $31 million redlining settlement with LA-based City National Bank* [online]. NPR. Available at: https://www.npr.org/2023/01/12/1148751006/redlining-city-national-bank-doj-settlement.

Balk, G. (2020). Percentage of Black residents in Seattle is at its lowest point in 50 years. *Seattle Times.* [online] Available at: https://www.seattletimes.com/seattle-news/data/percentage-of-blacks-living-in-seattle-at-lowest-point-in-50-years/.

Ballentine, C. and Cachero, P. (2022). *Parents are buying homes for kids priced out of the housing market* [online]. Bloomberg.com. Available at: https://www.bloomberg.com/news/articles/2022-06-07/how-are-young-us-buyers-affording-homes-with-their-parents-money#xj4y7vzkg [Accessed 10 Jul. 2023].

Bowser, M. (2022). *Mayor Bowser announces a new goal to increase Black homeownership by 20,000 homeowners by 2030* [online]. Government of the District of Columbia: Muriel Bowser, Mayor. Available at: https://mayor.dc.gov/release/mayor-bowser-announces-new-goal-increase-black-homeownership-20000-homeowners-2030.

Broady, K., McComas, M., and Ouazad, A. (2021). *An analysis of financial institutions in Black-majority communities: Black borrowers and depositors face considerable challenges in accessing banking services* [online]. Brookings. Available at: https://www.brookings.edu/articles/an-analysis-of-financial-institutions-in-black-majority-communities-black-borrowers-and-depositors-face-considerable-challenges-in-accessing-banking-services/ [Accessed 10 Jul. 2023].

Choi, J. H. and Mattingly, P. J. (2022). *What different denial rates can tell us about racial disparities in the mortgage market* [online]. Urban Institute. Available at: https://www.urban.org/urban-wire/what-different-denial-rates-can-tell-us-about-racial-disparities-mortgage-market.

Detroit historical Society. (n.d.). *Race riot of 1943* [online]. Available at: https://detroithistorical.org/learn/encyclopedia-of-detroit/race-riot-1943#:~:text=Nine%20whites%20and%2025%20African.

Harvard T.H. Chan School of Public Health. (2023). *What's behind "shocking" U.S. life expectancy decline—and what to do about it* [online]. Harvard University. Available at: https://www.hsph.harvard.edu/news/hsph-in-the-news/whats-behind-shocking-u-s-life-expectancy-decline-and-what-to-do-about-it/#:~:text=April%2013%2C%202023%20%E2%80%93%20U.S.%20life.

Henderson, T. (2022). *Black families fall further behind on homeownership* [online]. Stateline. Available at: https://stateline.org/2022/10/13/black-families-fall-further-behind-on-homeownership/.

Honig, D. (2021). *Redlining in Seattle* [online]. www.historylink.org. Available at: https://www.historylink.org/File/21296.

Kelley, D., Majbouri, M., and Randolph, A. (2021). Black women are more likely to start a business than White men [online]. *Harvard Business Review*. Available at: https://hbr.org/2021/05/black-women-are-more-likely-to-start-a-business-than-white-men.

Leidy, L. (2023). *The future of homebuying: Does Gen Z have it even tougher than millennials?* [online]. Yahoo. Available at: https://www.yahoo.com/now/future-homebuying-does-gen-z-201732049.html?guce_referrer=aHR0cHM6Ly93d3cuZ29vZ2xlLmNvbS8&guce_referrer_sig=AQAAANPBWvXZNEkADxjfl-zaaqyi3Sc0DLk6TKP7mXA87anCwKf6xcNRGbXIsXHYj3K_QchT--EK0k0Vh9u-2wMJfRWEX55AFaOkMG9dU0IgJa3w_Z4SBO2xAFk4uwbJICuj3e46szIjtZRSFme2tUfXGl2OY-XsnWeGb9MGEg_3XAfI&guccounter=2.

Lilien, J. (2022). *Faulty foundations: Mystery-shopper testing in home appraisals exposes racial bias undermining black wealth* [online]. NCRC. Available at: https://ncrc.org/faulty-foundations-mystery-shopper-testing-in-home-appraisals-exposes-racial-bias-undermining-black-wealth/ [Accessed 10 Jul. 2023].

McIntosh, K., Moss, E., Nunn, R., & Shambaugh, J. (2020). *Examining the Black-White wealth gap* [online]. Brookings. Available at: https://www.brookings.edu/articles/examining-the-black-white-wealth-gap/.

National Day Archives. (n.d.). *National Black family business day* [online]. National Day Archives. Available at: https://www.nationaldayarchives.com/day/national-black-family-business-day/#:~:text=August%2026th%20of%20each%20calendar [Accessed 5 Jul. 2023].

Rothwell, J. and Perry, A. M. (2022). *How racial bias in appraisals affects the devaluation of homes in majority-Black neighborhoods* [online]. Brookings. Available at: https://www.brookings.edu/articles/how-racial-bias-in-appraisals-affects-the-devaluation-of-homes-in-majority-black-neighborhoods/#:~:text=Using%20self%2Dreported%20census%20valuations [Accessed 10 Jul. 2023].

Taylor, J. (2018). *15 most important assets that will increase your net worth* [online]. GOBankingRates. Available at: https://www.gobankingrates.com/money/financial-planning/important-assets-increase-money/.

TSL Contributor. (2022). "I might be able to pay you now": Mike Tyson inadvertently reveals how he's dodged paying millions in taxes to the IRS [online]. *Atlanta Black Star*. Available at: https://www.yahoo.com/now/might-able-pay-now-mike-180500277.html#:~:text=It%20forced%20Mike%20Tyson%20to [Accessed 10 Jul. 2023].

US Bank. (2023). *Two years later, U.S. Bank Access Commitment recognizes milestones* [online]. Available at: https://www.usbank.com/about-us-bank/company-blog/article-library/two-years-later-us-bank-access-commitment-recognizes-milestones.html#:~:text=U.S.%20Bank%20started%20with%20the [Accessed 10 Jul. 2023].

US Census Bureau. (2021). *Data on minority-owned, veteran-owned and women-owned businesses* [online]. Available at: https://www.census.gov/newsroom/press-releases/2021/annual-business-survey.html.

Vance, T. (2019). *Addressing mental health in the Black community.* [online] Columbia University Department of Psychiatry. Available at: https://www.columbiapsychiatry.org/news/addressing-mental-health-black-community#:~:text=Research%20Surrounding%20the%20Black%20Community.

Weinstein, J. (n.d.). *How to really address job and career satisfaction* [online]. Available at: https://www.dclifecounseling.com/how-to-address-career-dissatisfaction/#:~:text=Across%20America%2C%20only%2045%20percent,dead%20end%20in%20their%20career.

Wessler, M. (2022). *Updated charts provide insights on racial disparities, correctional control, jail suicides, and more* [online]. Prison Policy Initiative. Available at: https://www.prisonpolicy.org/blog/2022/05/19/updated_charts/.

Williams, V. (2021). *Women-owned employer businesses*. U.S. Small Business Administration.

worldpopulationreview.com. (n.d.). *Poorest cities in America* [online]. Available at: https://worldpopulationreview.com/us-city-rankings/poorest-cities-in-america.

Wright, T. C. (2022). *Women-owned businesses are on the rise* [online]. Samsung Business Insights. Available at: https://insights.samsung.com/2022/10/20/women-owned-businesses-are-on-the-rise/.

www.in2013dollars.com. (n.d.). *Housing price inflation, 1967→2022* [online]. Available at: https://www.in2013dollars.com/Housing/price-inflation/1967-to-2022?amount=100000 [Accessed 10 Jul. 2023].

Zalis, S. (2021). Black female entrepreneurs are launching more businesses than ever. *Forbes* [online]. Available at: https://www.forbes.com/sites/shelleyzalis/2021/05/25/black-female-entrepreneurs-are-launching-more-businesses-than-ever-heres-what-they-need-to-help-them-mature/?sh=731c589e6bc0 [Accessed 10 Jul. 2023].

INDEX

NOTES

_____

_____

_____

_____

_____

_____

_____

_____

_____

_____

_____

_____

_____

_____

_____

_____

_____

_____

_____